a homework manual for biblical living

wayne a. mack

vol. 2 family and marital problems

PUBLISHING

P.O. BOX 817 • PHILLIPSBURG • NEW JERSEY 08865-0817

PRINTED IN THE UNITED STATES OF AMERICA

ISBN 0-87552-357-9

CONTENTS

INTRODUCTION

In recent years it has been my privilege to lecture to church leaders in various parts of the United States on the subject of Biblical counseling. I have frequently told church leaders that God has given us in His Son, in His Spirit, and in His Word resources for helping people that no non-Christian counselor has. Consequently, I have suggested that we who are Christians should not run from the ministry of counseling but rather should welcome it and heartily engage in it.

After these lectures I have had many church leaders come to me and say, "I wholeheartedly agree with you and I am studying the Scriptures and other writings about Biblical counseling to become more competent to counsel. I believe I am improving and becoming more skillful in helping people with their problems, but there is one area where I find myself in need of much help. I know that the counseling session is not the 'magic hour' where the expert solves problems and changes people. I know that I must give people good Biblical homework that will hasten their improvement and help them to find their own solutions to problems. But that's my problem. I sometimes don't know what homework to give. Could you recommend a book that gives specific examples and samples of the kind of homework I might give to people with different kinds of problems?"

When asked this question, I have responded by saying that there are some samples of good homework in the various books written by Dr. Jay E. Adams and also in a marriage manual which I wrote, entitled, *Strengthening Your Marriage* (Presbyterian and Reformed Publishing Company). Many of these men have replied, "I know about these resources, but would like to have more. Please give some thought to producing a book that would provide more suggestions."

Well, this manual, along with volume 1, is an attempt to provide the "more" which has been requested. Included in this manual are homework assignments designed to help people overcome various marriage and family problems. I have personally used this material with counselees and have seen God use it to help people to discover from His Word how to overcome many serious problems.

The homework assignments in this manual, as well as those included in volume 1, have been developed throughout the years I have been involved in counseling. A few of them were given to me by other men (wherever I know the donor, he is acknowledged). One or two may be a combination and adaptation of insights gleaned from various sources that I do not remember. Most of them were developed by me to meet the existing needs of my counselees.

This homework manual will supplement the material in *Strengthening Your Marriage* and should be used in conjunction with that book. It may also be used as a study guide for a series of tapes on *Strengthening Your Marriage,* by Wayne Mack. These tapes may be purchased from Christian Study Services, 1790 E. Willow Grove Ave., Laverock, Pa. 19118, or Biblical Counseling and Living Supplies, 2154 Hill Road, Sellersville, Pa. 18960, or by calling (215) 433-8272.

Wayne A. Mack

Section One

HOMEWORK

FOR

HUSBANDS AND/OR WIVES

COUNSELING ASSIGNMENT

1. *Have at least four family conferences of at least 45 minutes each* between now and your next session. (On the days when you don't meet to specifically do your assignments, make sure you do have a time when you can relate and share with one another.) Remember, 45 minutes four times a week is only three hours out of 168. Your marriage is certainly worth that. *Observe the following rules in your conferences:*

   a. Agree upon a place and time when you will meet. The place should provide the atmosphere in which free and uninterrupted discussion may occur. The time should be set and kept.

   b. Read Ephesians 4:17-32 before conferring on the first two days and I Corinthians 13:1-8 before conferring on the last two days. Seek to conduct your conferences and all of your life according to the principles laid down in these passages.

   c. Ask God to help you do His will in your conferences and entire life.

   d. Speak the truth in love. Do not argue, defend yourself, raise your voice, interrupt, or lose your cool. The conference table is a place to confer and discuss, not to attack, malign, get revenge, or argue. It is a place to uncover and solve problems, not to make or compound problems. If any conferee argues, explodes, clams up, becomes abusive or highly emotional, the other person should rise and stand quietly (not speaking a word). This pre-arranged and pre-agreed-upon signal should be used only if a conferee is really violating the aforementioned rules of the family conference. It must not be used as a means of "copping out" and refusing to face the issues. Remember, you will never solve problems by ignoring or evading them. They must be uncovered and confronted before any solution can come. If in the opinion of one conferee the other conferee is violating conference rules, the other conferee should indicate his willingness to change and go back to proper discussion. He/she must not debate or discuss the validity of the other person's judgment. He/she should ask God for help (silently) and quiet down and go back to discussion. If it becomes obvious that you are not ready to continue conferring according to biblical principle, the conference should be suspended for an hour or two or until the next session. In the meanwhile, think of how you may be a better partner, a better communicator, a better problem solver. Force yourself to see things from the other person's point of view. Sit where he/she sits. Think as he/she thinks. Then come back together again and proceed. Sometimes physical exercise will help you to control yourself. Go to God in prayer. Think of the Scriptures listed under *b* above.

3

e. Have the husband, as head of the home, lead the conferences and the wife keep a record of what is done at the conferences.

2. At your first conference *read through this assignment sheet* in its entirety.

3. At your first conference read *What Do You Do When Your Marriage Goes Sour? Discuss the two main concepts of love and forgiveness* presented in this pamphlet. *Fill out the reading questionnaire* that your counselor gave you.

4. After you have finished nos. 2 and 3, if you still have time during your first conference, move on to begin to *make a list of your respective sins and failures.** If there is no time for this in the first session, begin and complete this list in the other three sessions. The husband should be the first to look at his life and acknowledge how he has failed and is failing. The wife should make a record of what is acknowledged. To make this list, examine every area of your life: church, spiritual, Bible reading, prayer, witnessing, family leadership, finances, speech, emotions, attitudes, use of time, physical, personal, work, recreational, parents, in-laws, friends, children, amusements, habits, manners, sex, cleanliness, orderliness, relations with and concern for other people, stubbornness, irritability, rudeness, laziness, cooperativeness, appreciation, unselfishness and generosity, decision making, etc. After the husband has finished acknowledging his failures, the wife should examine her life and acknowledge her faults audibly to the husband. Her faults should also be recorded. These lists should be very comprehensive and specific because they will reveal why you are having the problems you are having and how you must change. Don't be abstract and vague. For example, don't merely say, "I am inconsiderate or thoughtless," Rather say:

1) "I do not help my wife with the housework or dishes when she is tired or not feeling well."

2) "I do not do the fix-it jobs around the house that I know she wants done."

3) "I do not listen intently to him/her when he/she wants to talk about his/her problems and concerns. I give the impression that he/she is making mountains out of molehills."

4) "I do not schedule a time daily to talk and share with him/her and develop our friendship."

5) "I frequently criticize his/her parents or relatives."

6) "I do not plan regular fun times and recreation for us to do together. I go off and do my own thing or sit around and watch TV, but am not actively seeking to develop common interests and recreation."

7) "I leave the room or yell or cry or explode when trouble or disagreement arises about the use of money."

8) "I do not lead family devotions or I do not lead my family by making wise decisions."

---

* The "Log Lists" on pages 31-33 and 47-50 were developed to make this assignment very meaningful and helpful.

9) "I waste money on clothes or. . . ." "I spend impulsively."
When you have finished acknowledging your respective faults, the wife should add to the husband's list of faults things he has missed. The husband should then do the same for his wife. Do not argue or defend yourself; just write down what is said and we will deal with these things later.

5. Fill out the "Rate Your Marriage Inventory" given to you by your counselor. Share your inventory with your spouse, but don't get into an emotional discussion about what is on your respective forms. Try to understand the problems from your partner's viewpoint. During the counseling sessions we will give specific homework to help you solve the problems.

6. *Bring your completed homework with you.* Your counselor knows from experience that success in counseling depends on how well you complete and apply your homework in this and succeeding sessions. Biblical counseling works when you and the counselor work. Your counselor commits himself to work and pray with you as long as you will make your counseling homework and its application a priority matter in your life. You will make progress and your life will be fuller very quickly if you will take your homework and its application to your life seriously.

READING REPORT FORM

A. Read _____

B. Write down the most important principles or insights presented by the author in this booklet.

C. Do you agree or disagree with the author? Put a check mark where you agree and where you disagree. If you disagree, give your reasons.

D. Evaluate or assess your life in the light of the insights presented in this booklet. Note where you are failing and where you are succeeding in implementing the truths of this booklet. What do you need to change? How will you go about making the changes?

COMMUNICATION WORKSHEET

A. List five things that you could discuss with your mate. Now plunge in and seek a good time to actually communicate.

B. Evaluate your conversation. (Perhaps you should make a tape recording of some of your ordinary family conversation. Then listen to yourself.) Answer the following questions about your conversation by using this rating scale: 0 = never, 1 = seldom, 2 = sometimes, 3 = frequently, 4 = always. Circle the questions where improvement is needed.

1. Do you really show an interest in what others are saying (_____) or are you interested only in what you are talking about? _____

2. Are you a know-it-all? _____

3. Is your voice pleasant, gentle, and friendly? _____

4. Do you say things clearly and simply so that others can understand?_____ Are you lovingly honest or evasive and untrue? _____ Are you open or secretive?_____ Do you often send backdoor messages? _____

5. Are you predominantly appreciative and affirmative (_____) or critical and negative? _____

6. Do you encourage others (_____) or belittle them? _____

7. Is your family better because of your involvement with them?_____ How?

8. Does your family feel free to be honest and open with you? _____ Is it safe for them to tell you the truth about you as they see it (_____) or do they have to fear speaking the truth to you? _____

9. Do you tend to dominate a conversation in which you are involved? _____ Do you ever "whip into silence" by your tone or reaction? _____

10. Are you willing to listen to opinions that are different from yours and not be threatened by them? _____ Are you a highly opinionated, prejudiced person? _____

11. When others want to talk to you, do you give them your undivided attention (_____) or are you usually too busy? _____

12. Do you consider communication with your family to be a priority matter? _____ Is it more important to you than watching TV? _____ Than reading the newspaper? _____ Than going fishing? _____ Than taking a nap? _____ If you had to choose between talking to your family and doing one of the aforementioned things, would you usually choose talking to your family? _____

13. Are you often not in the mood to talk? _____ Do you give in to your moods (_____) or deny yourself and focus on the needs of others? _____

14. Are you frequently sarcastic and nasty in your speech (_____) or do you usually use wholesome gracious, considerate, and respectful speech? _____

15. Are you usually cheerful and bright (＿＿) or overly serious and somber? ＿＿ Do you usually have a merry heart (＿＿) or a sullen spirit? ＿＿
16. Do you nag? ＿＿
17. Do you lecture or moralize?
18. Do you sometimes exaggerate problems, or the other person's faults, etc? ＿＿
19. Do you sometimes mindread, read into the other person's words and accuse him/her of meaning things he/she didn't really say? ＿＿
20. Do you insist on having the last word? ＿＿
21. Do you make time to communicate on a daily basis? ＿＿
22. Do you often bring up the other person's past mistakes? ＿＿
23. Do you often refuse the other person's suggestions or advice without really thinking about what he/she is saying? ＿＿

C. Study the following verses; ask God what they say about communication; write down what they say and how you need to apply them in your circumstances. Use another sheet of paper if you need more space to answer.

1. Matthew 12:34-37: ＿＿＿＿＿＿＿＿＿＿＿＿＿＿＿＿＿＿

＿＿＿＿＿＿＿＿＿＿＿＿＿＿＿＿＿＿＿＿＿＿＿＿＿＿

2. Ephesians 4:25-27: ＿＿＿＿＿＿＿＿＿＿＿＿＿＿＿＿＿

＿＿＿＿＿＿＿＿＿＿＿＿＿＿＿＿＿＿＿＿＿＿＿＿＿＿

3. Ephesians 4:29-32: ＿＿＿＿＿＿＿＿＿＿＿＿＿＿＿＿＿

＿＿＿＿＿＿＿＿＿＿＿＿＿＿＿＿＿＿＿＿＿＿＿＿＿＿

4. Ephesians 5:18, 19: ＿＿＿＿＿＿＿＿＿＿＿＿＿＿＿＿＿

＿＿＿＿＿＿＿＿＿＿＿＿＿＿＿＿＿＿＿＿＿＿＿＿＿＿

5. Colossians 4:6: ＿＿＿＿＿＿＿＿＿＿＿＿＿＿＿＿＿＿＿

＿＿＿＿＿＿＿＿＿＿＿＿＿＿＿＿＿＿＿＿＿＿＿＿＿＿

6. II Timothy 2:24, 25: ＿＿＿＿＿＿＿＿＿＿＿＿＿＿＿＿

＿＿＿＿＿＿＿＿＿＿＿＿＿＿＿＿＿＿＿＿＿＿＿＿＿＿

7. Titus 3:1, 2: ＿＿＿＿＿＿＿＿＿＿＿＿＿＿＿＿＿＿＿＿

＿＿＿＿＿＿＿＿＿＿＿＿＿＿＿＿＿＿＿＿＿＿＿＿＿＿

8. I Peter 3:10, 11: ＿＿＿＿＿＿＿＿＿＿＿＿＿＿＿＿＿＿

＿＿＿＿＿＿＿＿＿＿＿＿＿＿＿＿＿＿＿＿＿＿＿＿＿＿

9. James 1:19, 20: _____

10. Proverbs 12:25; 15:1; 15:28; 17:14; 20:5; 25:9, 11, 12, 15: _____

11. Proverbs 12:16, 18; 15:5; 16:21, 24, 27; 17:9; 18:6, 13, 17, 23: _____

D. Select two or three areas in which you need to improve to become a better communicator with your family. Confess your failure to God in this area, ask Him to help you to change and then go to work on them. Begin every day by reaffirming your desire to change, ask God for help, memorize Scripture that speaks to the practice you want to change, and deliberately throughout the day seek to be different. At the end of every day, review your progress, ask God for forgiveness where you have failed, and again commit yourself to becoming different in the areas you are seeking to change. Write out the changes you want to make and plan how you will bring them to pass. Here are two examples of the type of changes you might want to make:
   1. I'm too serious and somber and need to be more cheerful and bright. I will take to heart Philippians 4:8; Proverbs 15:13; 16:24; and Ephesians 5:18, 19.
   2. I have not made family communication a priority matter. I will take and make time every day to listen and talk to my family. I will judiciously ask others about their concerns and interests. I will turn off TV or put down the newspaper when someone wants to talk. I will communicate to them that talking and listening to them is really important to me.
E. List three times when you have not communicated well. In the light of the above, analyze these incidents to see what you did wrong and how you should have handled them differently.
F. Take the following list as headings, list three items under each in order of priority as you believe your mate would respond. His/her joys, disappointments, goals, likes, dislikes, interests, concerns. Ask your mate to check your knowledge of him/her.
G. List ten fun things your mate enjoys that you may enjoy with him/her. Plan to do at least one thing every week.
H. Make a list of what (actions, attitudes, qualities, traits, abilities, etc.) you appreciate about him/her. Continue to add to this list on a regular basis. Regularly express appreciation to the other person for the things you appreciate about him/her. Focus on these things instead of what you don't like (Phil. 4:8).

9

COMMUNICATION GUIDELINES

(These communication guidelines were provided by Timothy Keller.)

Proverbs 18:21; 25:11; Job 19:2; James 3:8-10; I Peter 3:10; Ephesians 4:25-32

Think about the guidelines and study the supporting Scripture verses. Rate yourself on each of these items: Excellent (3), Good (2), Fair (1), Poor (0).

1. *Be a ready listener* and do not answer until the other person has finished talking (Prov. 18:13; James 1:19). _____
2. *Be slow to speak.* Think first. Don't be hasty in your words. Speak in such a way that the other person can understand and accept what you say (Prov. 15:23, 28; 29:20; James 1:19). _____
3. *Don't go to bed angry!* Each day clear the offenses of that day. Speak the truth always, but do it in love. Do not exaggerate (Eph. 4:15, 25; Col. 3:8; Matt. 6:34). _____
4. *Do not use silence to frustrate the other person.* Explain why you are hesitant to talk at this time (Prov. 15:28; 16:21, 23; 10:19; 18:2; Col. 4:6; Prov. 20:15). _____
5. *Do not become involved in quarrels.* It is possible to disagree without quarreling (Prov. 17:14; 20:3; Rom. 13:13; Eph. 4:31). _____
6. *Do not respond in uncontrolled anger.* Use a soft and kind response and tone of voice (Prov. 14:29; 15:1; 25:15; 29:11; Eph. 4:26, 31). _____
7. *When you are in the wrong, admit it and ask for forgiveness* and ask how you can change (James 5:16; Prov. 12:15; 16:2; 21:2, 29; 20:6; Matt. 5:23-25; Luke 17:3). _____
8. *When someone confesses to you, tell him/her you forgive him/her.* Be sure it is forgiven and not brought up to the person, to others, or to *yourself!* (Prov. 17:9; Eph. 4:32; Col. 3:13; I Pet. 4:8). _____
9. *Avoid nagging* (Prov. 10:19; 17:9; 16:21, 23; 18:6, 7; 27:15; 21:19). _____
10. *Do not blame or criticize the other person.* Instead, restore . . . encourage . . . edify (Rom. 14:13; Gal. 6:1; I Thess. 5:11).
11. *If someone verbally attacks, criticizes, or blames you, do not respond in the same manner* (Rom. 12:17, 21; I Pet. 2:23; 3:9)._____
12. *Try to understand the other person's opinion.* Make allowances for differences (Prov. 18:2, 13, 15; Phil. 3:15, 16). _____
13. *Be concerned about the interests of others* (Phil. 2:3; Eph. 4:2; Rom. 12:15). _____

What you have just studied are biblical directives for promoting good communication and good relationships with other people. To really put some teeth into your effort to become more biblical in your communicating, you may want to sign the following agreement to implement these guidelines. (If husband and wife, both sign.)

Name ——————————————————— Date ———————————

Name ——————————————————— Date ———————————

COMMUNICATION IMPROVEMENT EXERCISE

1. Communication exercise
   a. Visualize in your mind an automobile. Each person jot down two adjectives to describe it as you visualize it. Do the same for a chair, a house, a father, a good time, love.
   b. Share your notes with someone else. How much do your mental images differ? (Do with mate if you have a mate.)
   c. What does this tell you about communication?
2. What attitudes or messages do the following sentences convey to you? Do they convey respect, appreciation, consideration, encouragement, affection, and love, or disdain, disrespect, rudeness, animosity, hostility, rejection? Try to imagine yourself hearing these sentences from someone else.
   "You don't really care."
   "I really need you."
   "Well, what do you have to complain about today?"
   "It sounds as though you had a difficult day. Is there any way I can help you?"
   "You shouldn't feel that way!"
   "I'm really sorry that you feel that way. How can I help? I'll be glad to pray for you and do anything I can."
   "You never kiss me."
   "Do you know what, honey? I really love you and like to have you hold me and kiss me."
   "Well, what do you know? Miracles still happen. You're ready on time."
   "Hey, hon, I just wanted you to know that I really appreciated the way you hurried to be ready to go on time."
   "Honey, you're terrific and getting better all the time."
   "You always forget what I ask you to do."
   "I like the way you smile. It really brightens my day."
   "We ought to have company more often. It's the only time we get good food around here."
   "That was a super meal. You are a fantastic cook."
   "How comes you could get home early tonight when you don't do it other nights?"
   "Boy, it's really great you got home early. I really miss you during the day."

3. Reflect on the 13 guidelines for communication above and:
   a. List the items that you most need to work on changing.
   b. Write down two specific actions you can take to improve these items.
   c. Share these with your mate and ask for help in changing. Get other suggestions concerning how you can improve these items. If you do not have a mate, share with a close Christian friend.

WHAT THE BIBLE SAYS ABOUT
WRONG WORDS, GOOD WORDS—
IMPROVING YOUR SPEECH

Homework:

A. Study the verses below and make four lists:
   1. The kind of speech that is to be avoided.
   2. The kind of speech that is to be used by the Christian.
   3. Look at list no. 1 and write down the specific ways you have been failing in your speech.
   4. Look at list no. 2 and make a list of the specific kinds of words and speech you ought to do more.
B. Choose several verses that are relevant to you and work on memorizing them. Repeat them several times a day.
C. Review lists three and four at least two times a day. Seek to change daily.

Proverbs 10:12, 14, 17, 18, 19, 21, 32
Proverbs 10:6, 8, 10, 11
Proverbs 11:9, 11, 12, 13
Proverbs 12:6, 13, 16, 18
Proverbs 13:3
Proverbs 14:3, 17, 29
Proverbs 15:1-4, 18, 23, 28
Proverbs 16:21, 23, 24, 27, 28, 32
Proverbs 17:9, 14, 27-28
Proverbs 18:6-8, 13, 17, 21, 23
Proverbs 19:11, 13, 19, 23
Proverbs 20:3, 25
Proverbs 21:23
Proverbs 22:24-25
Proverbs 24:1, 2, 29, 28
Proverbs 25:8, 21-23, 25, 28
Proverbs 26:17-22
Proverbs 27:2
Proverbs 28:25
Proverbs 29:11, 20, 22
Proverbs 30:32, 33
Ecclesiastes 5:3
Ephesians 4:29, 30-32; 5:19-20
James 1:19, 26; 3:2-12
Matthew 12:34-37
Galatians 5:19-21, 22, 23, 15, 16
Colossians 3:17; 4:6
Psalm 19:13, 14
Philippians 4:8

13

COMMON INTERESTS AND ACTIVITIES

How do you and your spouse take part in the following activities?
(Check appropriate space)

	Together	Both but not together	One Exclusively	Primarily	Neither
Church (attendance and service)					
Reading					
Competitive sports (tennis, etc.)					
Spectator sports					
Outdoor activities (camping, fishing, walking, etc.)					
Social gatherings (family, friends, church, community, etc.)					
Clubs, organizations					
Art appreciation (listening to music, visiting museums, etc.)					
Creative and interpretive art (writing, painting, performing)					
Hobbies (collecting, gardening, sewing, woodwork, etc.)					
Business and professional activity					
School functions or organizations					
Politics					
Motion pictures					
Family devotions					
Vacations					
Shopping					
Table games					
Sightseeing (traveling)					
Extending hospitality					
Other					

COMPANIONSHIP RECORD

Directions: Keep record of time spent with _____ and what you do.

Day	Record of time	What you do
Sunday		
Monday		
Tuesday		
Wednesday		
Thursday		
Friday		
Saturday		

HANDLING FAMILY FINANCES

A. Discuss and record your personal views about:
1. The basis on which you will select your occupation and place of employment;
2. Credit buying, charge accounts, and loans;
3. Savings accounts and investments;
4. Giving to the church, needy people, parents, and children;
5. Spending money on amusements, entertainment, recreation, and vacations;
6. Financial planning, budgeting, and bookkeeping;
7. The husband working overtime or having a second job;
8. Having a job that requires you to work evenings and/or be away from home for extended periods of time;
9. The wife taking a job;
10. Financial priorities (furniture or automobile, husband's clothing or wife's, etc.);
11. Insurance;
12. Making out a will;
13. Providing for emergencies;
14. Who will pay the bills and handle routine financial affairs;
15. Buying or spending without the other person's agreement;
16. Providing for old age;
17. Going out for dinner;
18. Personal allowances;
19. Buying or renting a home;
20. Joint or separate bank accounts;
21. Spending money on gifts for each other;
22. How much should be spent on clothes, furniture, automobiles, hobbies, etc.

B. Discuss and record the attitudes your respective parents had toward money. Were they savers or spenders? Were they conscientious about paying bills? Did they budget their money? Did they spend money for luxuries or only for necessities? Were they generous in giving to the church and others? Was making money a major focus of their lives? Did they make joint decisions about money? Did your mother have money apportioned to her for spending? Who was in charge of the finances? Did they keep good records? Did your mother work? Did they have joint or separate bank accounts? Did they have a savings account, insurance, or investments? Did they buy new automobiles or furniture frequently? Did they frequently repaint or redecorate? Were they self-producers? (Evaluate how your respective parents differed and where your attitudes and financial outlook is like theirs and different from your mate's. Your differing viewpoints may be fertile soil for bitterness, irritation, and resentment unless you can come to a mutually satisfying agreement. Discuss how you can resolve your differences.)

C. List a number of truths about finances found in:

Psalm 24:1: _____

I Chronicles 29:11, 12: _____

Proverbs 11:24, 25, 28: _____

Proverbs 12:10: _____

Proverbs 13:11: _____

Proverbs 10:4: _____

Proverbs 13:18, 24: _____

Proverbs 15:16, 17, 22: _____

Proverbs 16:8, 16: _____

I Thessalonians 4:10-12: _____

Ephesians 4:28: _____

I Timothy 6:3-10, 17-18: _____

Proverbs 3:9, 10: _____

Luke 14:28: _____

Proverbs 6:6-8: _____

Proverbs 21:5: _____

Proverbs 16:3: _____

Romans 13:6-8: _____

Proverbs 27:23, 24: _____

Proverbs 20:18: _____

Proverbs 29:22: _____

D. Several of the aforementioned Scripture verses emphasize the importance of financial planning or budgeting. Use the following form to work out a budget for your family.

FINANCES

Estimated Income	*Yearly*	*Monthly*
Take-home pay	_____	_____
Other income (dividends, interest, etc.)	_____	_____
TOTAL	_____	_____

Estimated Expenses (Check last year's
records and anticipate any increases)
    Fixed Expenses

	Yearly	*Monthly*
Contributions	_____	_____
Housing (rent, mortgage, phone, heat, electricity, water, sewer, garbage)	_____	_____
Insurance (property, life, health, auto, etc.)	_____	_____
Taxes (property, school, other)	_____	_____
Debts or loans other than mortgage	_____	_____
Savings or investments	_____	_____
TOTAL	_____	_____

    Flexible Expenses

	Yearly	*Monthly*
Family expenses (medical & dental care, clothing, vacation & travel, education, recreation, Christmas & other gifts, children's allowances, haircuts)	_____	_____
Expenses of wife (groceries, household operation, personal, cleaning & laundry, newspaper, other)	_____	_____
Expenses of husband (operation & maintenance of auto, personal, professional or union dues, books & journals	_____	_____
Home maintenance (house & furnishings)	_____	_____

18

Emergencies	_____	_____
Miscellaneous	_____	_____
TOTAL	_____	_____
TOTAL INCOME	_____	_____
— TOTAL EXPENSES	_____	_____
+ or —	_____	_____

If expenses exceed your income, you must either decrease your expenses or increase your income. Write out what you will do and how you will do it.

MARRIAGE HOMEWORK

Supply the requested information for the following items:

1. My marriage would be better if only

    a. _____

    b. _____

    c. _____

    d. _____

2. In specific terms, list 10 things you have done to make your marriage a success.
3. In specific terms, what do you expect out of marriage? What are your goals in marriage? What do you expect from your partner?
4. In specific terms, list 10 ways you have been at fault in your marriage.
5. In specific terms, list 10 ways you may change to make your marriage a better marriage.
6. In specific terms, list 15 ways that you and your mate differ in attitude, actions, behavior, interests, desires, goals, mannerisms, etc.
7. In specific terms, using specific instances if possible, write out in detail how you show it when you are angry, hurt, opposed, criticized, or denied.
8. In specific terms, write out what you would ask Jesus Christ to change about your marriage if you were assured He would work a miracle and do it.
9. Honestly evaluate the changes you would like to see in your mate. Are they really important? Do you have biblical grounds for desiring these changes? Are they for the good of your mate or just because you want them? Are you really concerned about your mate or just having your own way and making it easy on yourself?
10. Consider Philippians 2:3, 4 and Ephesians 4:1-3 and write out 10 specific ways in which you may demonstrate to your mate that you think he/she is really important and that you are sincerely interested in the things that interest him/her.
11. List 10 things you do to please your mate.
12. List five things you should do more often.
13. List 10 things your mate does that please you.
14. List five things you would like your mate to do more frequently.

RATE YOUR MARRIAGE
(Wife)

Name _____

This test is designed to evaluate how you are doing in your marriage relationship and to spot problem areas so that you may work on correcting them. The test will be most beneficial if you and your husband both take it and then sit down and discuss your respective answers to each question. Seek to understand clearly the other person's reasons for answering each question as he/she did. If your answers pinpoint some difficulties, focus on how you could resolve the problem. Don't just attack or blame the other person. Remember, God does have a solution to every problem if you will handle your problems and seek to solve them in a biblical way. *Rating scale:* never = 0; seldom = 1; sometimes = 2; frequently = 3; always = 4. Write the number that describes what you judge to be true of your marriage on the blank following each question.

1. Does the fact that Jesus Christ is Lord manifest itself in practical ways in your marriage? _____
2. Do you use the Bible to determine your convictions, decisions and practices in life in general and marriage in particular? _____
3. Do you and your spouse study the Bible, pray, worship God, and seek to serve God together? _____
4. Do you and your spouse seek to please one another? _____
5. Do you ask for forgiveness when you have done something wrong? _____
6. Do you allow your mate to disagree with you or make a mistake without becoming nasty or punishing him/her? _____
7. Do you focus on the things you appreciate about your mate and express appreciation in tangible ways? _____
8. Do you communicate with one another on a daily basis? _____
9. Do you express your opinions, ideas, plans, aspirations, fears, feelings, likes, dislikes, views, problems, joys, frustrations, annoyances to each other?
10. Do you and your mate understand each other when you try to express yourselves? _____
11. Do you do many different things together and enjoy being with each other? Are you involved in common projects? _____
12. Do you show love in many practical and tangible ways? _____
13. Do you still court one another by occasional gifts, unexpected attention, etc.? _____
14. Is your conversation pleasant and friendly? _____

21

15. Do you pray for one another, support and seek to encourage one another? _____
16. Can you discuss differing viewpoints on values, priorities, religious convictions, politics, etc., without becoming irritated or upset? _____
17. Do you anticipate sexual relations with your partner? _____
18. Are your sexual desires compatible? _____
19. Do you freely discuss your sexual desires with your mate? _____
20. Do you agree about the way money should be spent? _____
21. Do you think your spouse is as concerned about your views about the way money should be spent as he/she is about his/her own? _____
22. Do you agree on how to bring up your children? _____
23. Do your children know that it is foolish to try to play one of you against the other; that if Dad say "no," Mother will agree, etc.? _____
24. Do you refuse to lie to your spouse; are you building your relationship on speaking the truth? Can your spouse put full confidence in whatever you say, knowing that you really mean what you say? _____
25. Do your have a good relationship with your in-laws? Do you appreciate them? _____
26. Do you really respect your spouse? _____
27. Are you glad to introduce your spouse to friends and associates? _____
28. Do you control yourself when you are moody so that you do not disrupt your family and inflict your moodiness on others? _____
29. Do you seek to change your specific habits that may cause discomfort or displeasure to your spouse? _____
30. Do you make your relationship with your spouse a priority matter? _____
31. Do you treat your mate with respect and dignity? _____
32. Do you accept corrective criticisms graciously? _____
33. Do you agree concerning the roles and responsibilities of the husband and wife? _____
34. Are you willing to face, discuss, and look for scriptural solutions to problems without blowing up or attacking the other person or dissolving into tears? _____
35. Do you maintain your own spiritual life through Bible study, prayer, regular church attendance, and fellowship with God's people? _____

Total _____

A perfect score for this test would be 140, and this, of course, is the ideal toward which every couple should strive. I would suggest that the couple that scores 95-140 probably has a good marriage where two people are experiencing unity and happiness. Even so, these people must not become complacent, but must continue to work and try to improve. This side of heaven there is always room for improvement. Marriages that score 70-94 reveal the need for improvement. Couples in this bracket should note the areas where improvement is needed (indicated by this test) and immediately make changes. Marriages that score 69 or below are in need of great improvement. Your marriage is far below the biblical norm, and this explains why you are not experiencing unity or fulfillment in marriage. The two of you need to sit down and discuss your problems and then work out a biblical plan to solve them. God has a solution in His Word for every problem if you will seek it and apply it. Your marriage can be different. God says it can. The Holy Spirit can help you to make it so. But remember, God often uses godly men to assist His people (Prov. 11:14; 12:15; 15:22). Perhaps the two of you should seek counsel from a wise and godly counselor.

To make this test accurate and, consequently, of maximum value, you ought to be able to support the way you scored each question with specific examples or reasons from your own experience. If you cannot support your score with evidence, your score is suspect.

RATE YOUR MARRIAGE
(Husband)

Name _____

This test is designed to evaluate how you are doing in your marriage relationship and to spot problem areas so that you may work on correcting them. The test will be most beneficial if you and your husband both take it and then sit down and discuss your respective answers to each question. Seek to understand clearly the other person's reasons for answering each question as he/she did. If your answers pinpoint some difficulties, focus on how you could resolve the problem. Don't just attack or blame the other person. Remember, God does have a solution to every problem if you will handle your problems and seek to solve them in a biblical way. *Rating scale:* never = 0; seldom = 1; sometimes = 2; frequently = 3; always = 4. Write the number that describes what you judge to be true of your marriage on the blank following each question.

1. Does the fact that Jesus Christ is Lord manifest itself in practical ways in your marriage? _____
2. Do you use the Bible to determine your convictions, decisions and practices in life in general and marriage in particular? _____
3. Do you and your spouse study the Bible, pray, worship God, and seek to serve God together? _____
4. Do you and your spouse seek to please one another? _____
5. Do you ask for forgiveness when you have done something wrong? _____
6. Do you allow your mate to disagree with you or make a mistake without becoming nasty or punishing him/her? _____
7. Do you focus on the things you appreciate about your mate and express appreciation in tangible ways? _____
8. Do you communicate with one another on a daily basis? _____
9. Do you express your opinions, ideas, plans, aspirations, fears, feelings, likes, dislikes, views, problems, joys, frustrations, annoyances to each other?
10. Do you and your mate understand each other when you try to express yourselves? _____
11. Do you do many different things together and enjoy being with each other? Are you involved in common projects? _____
12. Do you show love in many practical and tangible ways? _____
13. Do you still court one another by occasional gifts, unexpected attention, etc.? _____
14. Is your conversation pleasant and friendly? _____

15. Do you pray for one another, support and seek to encourage one another? ___

16. Can you discuss differing viewpoints on values, priorities, religious convictions, politics, etc., without becoming irritated or upset? ___

17. Do you anticipate sexual relations with your partner? ___

18. Are your sexual desires compatible? ___

19. Do you freely discuss your sexual desires with your mate? ___

20. Do you agree about the way money should be spent? ___

21. Do you think your spouse is as concerned about your views about the way money should be spent as he/she is about his/her own? ___

22. Do you agree on how to bring up your children? ___

23. Do your children know that it is foolish to try to play one of you against the other; that if Dad say "no," Mother will agree, etc.? ___

24. Do you refuse to lie to your spouse; are you building your relationship on speaking the truth? Can your spouse put full confidence in whatever you say, knowing that you really mean what you say? ___

25. Do your have a good relationship with your in-laws? Do you appreciate them? ___

26. Do you really respect your spouse? ___

27. Are you glad to introduce your spouse to friends and associates? ___

28. Do you control yourself when you are moody so that you do not disrupt your family and inflict your moodiness on others? ___

29. Do you seek to change your specific habits that may cause discomfort or displeasure to your spouse? ___

30. Do you make your relationship with your spouse a priority matter? ___

31. Do you treat your mate with respect and dignity? ___

32. Do you accept corrective criticisms graciously? ___

33. Do you agree concerning the roles and responsibilities of the husband and wife? ___

34. Are you willing to face, discuss, and look for scriptural solutions to problems without blowing up or attacking the other person or dissolving into tears? ___

35. Do you maintain your own spiritual life through Bible study, prayer, regular church attendance, and fellowship with God's people? ___

Total ___

A perfect score for this test would be 140, and this, of course, is the ideal toward which every couple should strive. I would suggest that the couple that scores 95-140 probably has a good marriage where two people are experiencing unity and happiness. Even so, these people must not become complacent, but must continue to work and try to improve. This side of heaven there is always room for improvement. Marriages that score 70-94 reveal the need for improvement. Couples in this bracket should note the areas where improvement is needed (indicated by this test) and immediately make changes. Marriages that score 69 or below are in need of great improvement. Your marriage is far below the biblical norm, and this explains why you are not experiencing unity or fulfillment in marriage. The two of you need to sit down and discuss your problems and then work out a biblical plan to solve them. God has a solution in His Word for every problem if you will seek it and apply it. Your marriage can be different. God says it can. The Holy Spirit can help you to make it so. But remember, God often uses godly men to assist His people (Prov. 11:14; 12:15; 15:22). Perhaps the two of you should seek counsel from a wise and godly counselor.

To make this test accurate and, consequently, of maximum value, you ought to be able to support the way you scored each question with specific examples or reasons from your own experience. If you cannot support your score with evidence, your score is suspect.

GOD'S BLUEPRINT FOR MARRIAGE
(Genesis 2:24)

DISCUSSION GUIDE

A. List three things you believe the Scripture means in Genesis 2:24.

1. _____

2. _____

3. _____

B. In Malachi 2:14 marriage is called a "covenant" or "contract." What implications does this have for the marriage relationship?

_____

_____

_____

C. In reference to marriage, Genesis 2:18 and Malachi 2:14 indicate that one of the purposes of marriage is companionship. Discuss what this means in specific terms and list five ways you are expressing and developing your companionship with one another.

D. Discuss your marriage in terms of leaving and cleaving and oneness.
1. Have you really left your parents? If not, how not?
2. Are you absolutely committed (cleaving) to your mate? Are you absolutely devoted and loyal?
3. Rate the intimacy level of your marriage. How much oneness do you have spiritually, recreationally, intellectually, sexually, etc.

E. Discuss and list what you can do to strengthen your marriage relationship.

1. _____

2. _____

3. _____

4. _____

5. _____

6. _____

27

F. Discuss and list your marriage goals. What do you want out of marriage?

1. _____

2. _____

3. _____

4. _____

5. _____

6. _____

SORTING OUT RESPONSIBILITIES

A Plan for Promoting Unity in Marriage
and Overcoming Marital Conflicts

Many times conflicts arise in marriages because there has been no clear delineation of responsibilities. Sometimes when everything is everybody's responsibility, everything becomes nobody's responsibility. Or everybody is trying to do the same thing and confusion, frustration, bitterness, and competitiveness are the result. One person has one view about how or when something should be done; and the other person has another; and neither is willing to yield. Or, one person always seems to do the yielding. This provides the soil in which sinful and unnecessary resentment and bitterness may develop.

Much of this conflict can be eliminated if clear lines of responsibility are delineated. *The husband under God is the head or manager of the home* (Eph. 5:22-27; I Tim. 3:4, 5). He is the one who is finally responsible to lovingly and biblically guide the home. The buck stops with him. *But he may decide to let his wife* (his chief helper—Gen. 2:18; Prov. 31:10-31) *take the leadership responsibility in certain areas.* Indeed, he will be wise to do this because she most certainly has more gifts and abilities and insight and experience in some areas than he does. In other areas, he will be more gifted and capable than she, and there he should take the lead in making decisions.

The husband and wife should share insights and advice in every area, but someone ought to be given the responsibility of seeing that things get done. Look over the following list and decide who will have the responsibility to plan and implement the different areas. Remember, some things are not right or wrong— just different ways of doing things or different ways of looking at something. In areas which are not vitally important or clearly spelled out by the Scriptures, be willing to defer to the other person. Don't make mountains out of molehills! Don't make everything a major issue! Talk matters over, assign responsibilities, make decisions, support each other, help carry out decisions.

This sorting out of responsibilities does not mean that a given area is one person's exclusive responsibility. It means that when a difference of opinion arises, one person has authority to make the choice. Certainly, in most areas a full and frank discussion will be conducted, all options and alternatives, pros and cons considered. However, when a conflict of opinion arises, someone must be allowed to make the decision, even if that decision is to wait until God brings the two of you into agreement. "If a house is divided against itself, that house will not be able to stand" (Mark 3:25, NASB).

In making a decision, make sure that you do not violate a biblical principle, seek the opinion and insight of your mate, ask God in prayer to guide you, believe that He will, consider and evaluate all options, and then, if you are the person who is responsible, make the decision. The other person should support the decision wholeheartedly and seek to make the decision a success unless it clearly violates biblical principle. Unity in marriage (Gen. 2:24) is tremendously important and should be maintained carefully. Following this plan is one way of promoting this unity. However, it will work only if both people agree to abide by it.

This "sorting out of responsibilities" does not mean the husband relinquishes his biblical responsibility to be the loving leader of the family. What it does mean is that he recognizes that God has given his wife certain abilities and capacities which may make her more competent in some areas than he is. Thus he delegates to her responsibilities which are in keeping with her resources. All the while, he maintains veto power, but he will not use it unless his wife's decisions clearly violate biblical principle.

Scripture declares: "[Love] is not rude; it is not self seeking" (I Cor. 13:5, NIV). "Make my joy complete by being like minded, having the same love, being one in spirit and purpose. Do nothing out of selfish ambition or vain conceit, but in humility consider others better than yourselves. Each of you should look not only to your own interests, but also to the interests of others" (Phil. 2:2-4, NIV). "Live in harmony with one another. Don't be proud, but be willing to associate with people of low position. Do not be conceited." "Be devoted to one another in brotherly love. Honor one another above yourselves" (Rom. 12:16, 10, NIV). "If you keep on biting and devouring each other, . . . you will be destroyed by each other." "You, my brothers, were called to be free. But do not use your freedom to indulge your sinful nature; rather serve one another in love" (Gal. 5:15, 13, NIV).

This "Sorting Out Responsibilities" plan is offered as a means of actualizing these Bible admonitions.

On the blank space following the descriptive phrase, indicate who will be mainly responsible for the area described:

1. *Children:*

Neatness _____	Rules and Regulations _____
Bedtimes _____	Activities _____
Discipline _____	Social life (friends, dating) _____
Clothing _____	Allowances (money management) _____
Chores _____	Manners _____
School work _____	TV watching _____

Hygiene _____ Spiritual life _____

Other (   ) _____ Other (   ) _____

2. *Money Management* (establishing budget) _____

3. *Financing* and *Bookkeeping* (paying bills, keeping records) _____

4. *Money raising* _____

5. *Purchasing food and household* _____

6. *Menu planning and cooking* (dietitian and chef) _____

7. *Housecleaning* _____

8. *Spiritual oversight* (church selection, attendance, family goals, family devotions, etc.) _____

9. *Family activities* (fun times, recreation, family projects, supervision of family nights) _____

10. *Vacation plans* _____

11. *Clothing purchasing* _____

12. *Clothing maintenance* _____

13. *Automobile* (selection, maintenance, etc.) _____

14. *Savings account* _____

15. *Hospitality* (friends in for dinner, etc.) _____

16. *Investment planning* _____

17. *Real estate purchases* (home selection, etc.) _____

18. *Gift planning and purchasing* _____

19. *Memorabilia keeping* (family records, pictures, newspaper clippings, letters, etc.) _____

20. *Family photography* _____

21. *Special events* (birthdays, anniversaries, etc.) _____

31

22. *Furniture* (selection, purchases, and maintaining) ——————————

23. *Time and schedule organizing* ———————————————

24. *Travel* (motels, maps, directions, etc.) ——————————————

25. *Retirement* (plans and provisions) ———————————————

26. *Yard work* ——————————————————————

27. *Gardening* ——————————————————————

28. *Family health services* ————————————————————

29. *Occupation, career* ————————————————————

Add any other responsibilities you can think of, under 30-32.

30. ————————————————————————————————

31. ————————————————————————————————

32. ————————————————————————————————

Section Two

HOMEWORK

FOR HUSBANDS

SAMPLE LOG LIST: HUSBAND AND FATHER

As mentioned in the title, this list is only a sample "log list." Go over it and personalize it. Make your own list, using this as a guideline. Be honest and objective and specific. Spare no punches. Be sure to add things that you see wrong in your life that are not mentioned on this list. Specifically confess your sins to God and those whom you have wronged. Seek God's help to change. Bring this list to your counselor.

Read Matthew 7:2-5; Romans 14:7-23; Ephesians 4:25-32; James 1:16; I John 1:9; Proverbs 28:13.

1. I do not lead family devotions regularly.

2. I fail to realize why _____ is so important to her.

3. I did not show enough concern in her interest in painting or _____.

4. I do not give enough assistance to her with _____ (examples).

5. For too long have I taken her love too much for granted.

6. I have often been irritable with her about _____ (examples).

7. I have been lazy in doing yard work.

8. I have been selfish sexually. In what ways?

9. I often expect her to drop housework and give me attention.

10. I become irritated when she is not ready to leave on time, but expect her to be patient when I am not ready on time.

11. I have not been giving her enough candy, flowers, gifts, and surprises.

12. I have not been keeping my desk neat and orderly.

13. I fail to express myself clearly and fully. I expect her to know.

14. I have been backward about showing any affection to my wife in public. In what ways?

15. My attention often wanders when she is talking to me.

16. I spend too much time away from home and am not available to her or the children many nights out of the week. Sometimes days go by without any significant communication between us.

17. I refuse to help her with the housework or dishes.

18. Sometimes I have a tendency to ask too many questions about a matter, wanting to know details out of foolish curiosity.

19. I have not helped enough with the _____ (give examples).

20. I sometimes initiate plans without her counsel (give examples).

21. I neglect odd jobs around the house. What odd jobs?

22. I sometimes tease her too much when with others. Examples?
23. I leave shoes, clothing, and other apparel lying around the house.
24. I selfishly play music too loudly.
25. I have not been exercising leadership in many areas of our marriage relationship (give examples).
26. I often grumble about taking the garbage out, even after it has been gathered up by her.
27. I complain about taking the dog for a walk even though I enjoy having a dog and she does most of the caring for it.
28. I haven't taken her shopping or other places often enough.
29. I should make more efforts to get along with her parents.
30. I am not as productive as I should be at work. In what ways?
31. I complain about the boss unfairly before others, and tend to exaggerate matters grossly. With whom and about what?
32. I am lazy when it comes to doing any study or work that will help me with my job.
33. I should be more thankful for God's mercy and blessings. Which ones?
34. I am backward about witnessing about Christ and frequently keep quiet when I should speak up. Give examples.
35. I am selfish and do not help others willingly when I have opportunity, although I often receive help from the same persons. Give examples.
36. I give in to depression rather than combat it.
37. I allow my attention to wander during church and get little benefit from worship and preaching.
38. I make plans without consulting God in prayer and the Word. Examples?
39. I should be more sensitive to her problems, moods, and feelings. I have not been as sympathetic as I should.
40. I seldom express appreciation or compliments to her.

41. I spend too much money on _____. Give examples.

42. I am too "tight" with money. In what ways?
43. I don't try to find things for us to do together.
44. I read the paper at mealtimes.
45. I don't kiss when I come or go.
46. I show too much interest in other women. How manifested? When? Where?
47. I accuse my wife of being frigid.
48. I drink too much.
49. I smoke too much.
50. I gamble too much.
51. I won't go to church with her.
52. I make excuses or often simply refuse to do what she wants to do. Examples?

53. I have bad manners. Examples?
54. I nag her about her faults or mistakes. Examples?
55. I act bored when I am home.
56. I am difficult to satisfy. In what areas?
57. I get angry or leave the room or refuse to talk when a problem or disagreement arises. About what? Give specifics.
58. I am too ambitious. About what? For what?
59. I make excuses or blame others when I make a mistake or do something wrong. Give examples.
60. I use profanity.
61. I don't seek help when we have serious problems. Give examples.
62. I don't trust. Whom? About what?
63. I am very untidy and disorganized. In what ways? Give specifics.
64. I become angry whenever she does not discipline the children as I want her to. Give examples.
65. I don't share my ideas and plans with her as much as I should. Give examples.
66. I don't give enough to the church. How much should you give?
67. I watch TV when my wife wants me to talk to her or go some place with her. Give examples if possible.
68. I don't spend time playing with the children.
69. I constantly criticize her family.
70. I get angry or hurt when she is too tired to have sexual relations.
71. I lose my temper and lash out when the children do not treat me with respect. Specifics?
72. I do not listen to her or the children without interrupting them.
73. I do not allow her or the children to have their own opinions without badgering them. I feel threatened whenever they disagree with me and try to pressure them into accepting my point of view.
74. I am not doing a good job as a Sunday school teacher. I don't study, visit, pray, or set the example I should be. How?
75. I have held a grudge against Pastor _____ or

    _____ for _____.
76. I insist that people perform or act in a certain way (my way) before I accept them.
77. I have criticized Pastor _____ or _____

    publicly without first going to him or making sure I had the facts. I haven't had the kind of love that covers a multitude of sins. Specifics?
78. I work too much and neglect my family and church. In what ways?
79. I am not using the gifts and abilities God has given me to glorify and serve Him as I ought. Which gifts?

80. I do not help other people very much. I am too much like the Levite or the priest in Luke 10, who saw needy people and ignored them. Examples?
81. I make threats with the children I don't keep and perhaps never even intended to keep. Examples?
82. I don't discipline the children effectively. How are you failing?
83. I am not teaching the children to live an orderly life. In what areas?
84. I am too rigid and demanding. Examples?
85. I hurt other people and don't like to ask for forgiveness. Examples?
86. I am not teaching the children to respect authority or fulfill responsibilities. I criticize my boss, disobey speed laws, etc.
87. I spend money on myself, but I am stingy with my wife and family.
88. I need to do more reading in areas that would help me to improve as a husband, father, and Christian.
89. I sometimes compare my wife and family unfavorably to other people. Examples if possible.
90. I do not cultivate my children's friendship enough.
91. I seldom believe their explanations for their actions or behavior. I am very suspicious of them and usually think the worst.
92. I take things too seriously and often make mountains out of molehills. I major on minors. Give examples if possible.
93. I have annoying habits and mannerisms. What are they?
94. I do not take care of myself physically as I should. Be specific.
95. I often neglect my wife's sexual needs and am mostly concerned about my own.
96. I still depend too much on my parents. I listen to them more than to my wife. Give examples.
97. I often make excessive demands upon my wife, expecting too much of her. Give examples.
98. I am sometimes a coward and do not lovingly stand up for what I know to be right. Give examples.

SCORE CARD FOR HUSBANDS

If you honestly evaluate yourself by this score card, you will be able to discern where you are failing and need to improve to be the husband God wants you to be. Suggestion: If you really want to know how you are doing, ask your wife to rate you.

Rating scale: never = 0; seldom = 1; sometimes = 2; frequently = 3; almost always = 4.

1. Do I love my wife and am I expressing biblical (unselfish) love to her as I should? _____

   Is my love an unconditional love? _____

   Do I love her even when I don't feel like it? _____

   Do I regularly express my love in words? _____

   Do I seek to provide for her varying desires (physical, emotional, intellectual, social, recreational, spiritual; for worth, appreciation, security, etc.)? _____

   Do I protect her (physically, spiritually, socially, emotionally)? _____

   Do I assist her with chores and responsibilities? _____

   Do I sacrifice for her? _____

   Do I freely share my life, my concerns, etc., with her? _____

   Do I regularly show appreciation? _____

   Do I put her first in my life after my relationship with God? _____

   Do I treat her with tenderness, respect, and courtesy? _____

   Do I fulfill her implied or unspoken desires and wishes? _____

   Do I frequently talk about her favorably in front of the children and other people? _____

   Do I remember birthdays, anniversaries, and other special occasions? _____

   Do I ask her advice frequently? _____

   Do I ask for forgiveness for failures quickly? _____

   Do I accept her suggestions without becoming upset? _____

   Do I change when she makes a suggestion? _____

   Do I handle the finances responsibly? _____

   Do I give her money to spend as she wishes? _____

   Do I run errands gladly? _____

   Do I take care of the children and let her do what she wants frequently? _____

   Do I give her my undivided attention when she wants to talk? _____

   Do I comfort and encourage her when she is hurt, fearful, anxious and weary? _____

Do I support her in her concerns and interests? ____

Do I plan to spend some time alone with her every day? ____

Do I change personal habits that annoy her? ____

Do I encourage her initiative and creativity? ____

Do I treat her as a very worthwhile person who is as important or more important than I am? ____

Do I really make my relationship with her a priority matter? ____

2. Take at least 10 of the questions that you answered with a 3 or 4 and give one or two examples of times you manifested love to your wife in these ways.

3. Select at least five ways in which you need to improve your expression of love to your wife. List these ways and plan what you will do to improve.

4. Am I a good manager? (I Tim. 3:4, 5; Eph. 5:23). Answer using 0-4 scale.

Do I know what is going on in my home from day to day? ____

Am I leading my family in the direction it is going? ____

Do I know the skills and abilities, strengths and weaknesses, problems and concerns of family members? ____

Do I use the skills of family members? ____

Do I have clearly defined goals for my family? ____

Do I motivate family members to use their skills and develop their abilities? ____

Do I lead in family worship regularly? ____

Do I spontaneously talk about spiritual matters? ____

Do I delegate responsibilities clearly? ____

Do I hold family members accountable for their responsibilities? ____

Do I have clear biblical convictions? ____

Have I made these convictions known in a specific way? ____

Do I set an example for my family in these convictions? ____

Do I have foresight in seeing potential problems and prepare my family for them? ____

Do I get along well with other family members and help them to get along with each other? ____

Do I spend time with family members regularly, listening to them, playing with them, encouraging them, communicating goals and directions to them? ____

Do I provide order and organization that give security? ____

Do I commend family members regularly? ____

Am I really in control of what is happening in my family? ____

Do I lead my family in church attendance and involvement? ___

Do I plan fun and recreational times for my family regularly? ___

Do I make decisions in a biblical way? ___

5. Take several of the questions that you answered with a 3 or 4 and give examples of how you lead your family in these areas.

6. Take several leadership areas where these questions revealed some weaknesses and plan what you will do to improve in these areas.

WAYS A HUSBAND MAY EXPRESS LOVE TO HIS WIFE

(How to Convince Your Wife You Love Her)

Evaluate the way you express love to your wife. Circle the ways you are neglecting. Ask your wife to go over the list and put a check mark in front of the ways she would like you to express love. Ask her to add other things to the list.

You may express love to your wife by—
1. Functioning as the loving leader of your home.
2. Frequently telling her you love her.
3. Giving her a regular amount of money to spend in any way she chooses.
4. Leading family devotions regularly.
5. Smiling and being cheerful when you come home from work.
6. Helping her wash and dry the dishes at least twice a week.
7. Taking care of the children for at least three hours every week so that she has free time to do whatever she wants.
8. Taking her out for dinner or to do some fun thing at least once a week.
9. Doing the "fix-it" jobs she wants done around the house.
10. Greeting her when you come home with a smile, a hug, a kiss, and an "Am I glad to see you. I really missed you today."
11. Giving her a lingering kiss.
12. Patting her on the shoulder or fanny or holding her hand or caressing her frequently.
13. Being willing to talk to her about her concerns and not belittle her for having those concerns.
14. Looking at her with an adoring expression.
15. Sitting close to her.
16. Rubbing her back or. . . .
17. Shaving or taking a bath or brushing your teeth before you have sex relations.
18. Wearing her favorite after-shave lotion.
19. Writing love notes or letters to her.
20. Letting her know you appreciate her and what you appreciate about her. Do this often and for things that are sometimes taken for granted. Pretend you are trying to convince her you think she is great and very important to you.
21. Doing the dishes while she relaxes or takes a bubble bath.
22. Fulfilling her implied or unspoken desires and wishes as well as the specific requests she makes of you. Anticipating what she might desire and surprising her by doing it before she asks.
23. Playing with her; sharing her hobbies and recreational preferences enthusiastically; including her in yours.
24. Seeking to set a good example before the children.

25. Talking about her favorably to the children when she can hear you and when she cannot.
26. Bragging about her good points as a wife in every other area to others; letting her know you are proud to have her as your wife.
27. Maintaining your own spiritual life through Bible study, prayer, regular church attendance and fellowship with with God's people.
28. Handling your affairs decently and in order; structuring your time and using it wisely.
29. Making plans prayerfully and carefully.
30. Asking her advice when you have problems or decisions to make.
31. Following her advice unless to do so would violate biblical principles.
32. Fulfilling your responsibilities.
33. Being sober, but not somber, about life.
34. Having a realistic, biblical, positive attitude toward life.
35. Discussing plans with your wife before you make decisions, and when the plans are made sharing them fully with your wife, giving reasons for making the decisions you did.
36. Thanking her in creative ways for her attempts to please you.
37. Asking forgiveness often and saying, "I was wrong and will try to change."
38. Actually changing where and when you should.
39. Sharing your insights, reading, good experiences with her.
40. Planning for a mini-honeymoon, where the two of you can do whatever you want to do.
41. Giving a low whistle or some other expression of admiration when she wears a new dress or your favorite negligee or. . . .
42. Gently brushing her leg under the table.
43. Being reasonably happy to go shopping with her.
44. Relating what happened at work or whatever you did apart from her.
45. Reminiscing about the early days of your marriage.
46. Expressing appreciation for her parents and relatives.
47. Taking her out to breakfast.
48. Agreeing with her about getting a new dress or some other item.
49. Thanking her when she supports your decisions and cooperates enthusiastically. Especially make it a matter of celebration when she supports and helps enthusiastically at times when you know she doesn't fully agree.
50. Asking her to have sexual relations with you and seeking to be especially solicitous of her desires. Express gratitude when she tries to please you.
51. Buying gifts for her.
52. Remembering anniversaries and other events that are special to her.
53. Watching the TV program or going where she wants to go instead of doing what you want to do. Do it cheerfully and enthusiastically.
54. Being cooperative and appreciative when she holds you, caresses or kisses you.
55. Being cooperative when she tries to arouse you and desires to have sexual relations. Never make fun of her for expressing her desires.

56. Running errands gladly.
57. Pampering her and making a fuss over her.
58. Being willing to see things from her point of view.
59. Being lovingly honest with her—no backdoor messages—no withholding of the truth that may hinder your present or future relationship.
60. Indicating you want to be alone with her and talk or just lie in each other's arms.
61. Refusing to "cop out" or "blow up" or attack or blameshift or withdraw or exaggerate when she seeks to make constructive suggestions or discuss problems.
62. Giving her your undivided attention when she wants to talk.
63. Cheerfully staying up past your bedtime to solve a problem or share her burdens.
64. Getting up in the middle of the night to take care of the children so that she may continue to sleep.
65. Holding her close while expressing tangible and vocal love when she is hurt, discouraged, weary, or burdened.
66. Planning vacations and trips with her.
67. Sometimes helping her yourself instead of telling the children to "help mommy."
68. Being eager to share a good joke or some other interesting information you have learned.
69. Joining with her in a team ministry in the church.
70. Doing a Bible study or research project together.
71. Establishing a family budget.
72. Keeping yourself attractive and clean.
73. Being cooperative, helpful, as a co-host when you have people in for dinner or fellowship.
74. Asking her to pray with you about something.
75. Spending time with the children in play, study, and communication.
76. Acknowledging that there are some specific areas or ways in which you need to improve.
77. Refusing to disagree with her in the presence of others.
78. Cooperating with her in establishing family goals and then in fulfilling them.
79. Being available and eager to fulfill her desires whenever and wherever possible and proper.
80. Beginning each day with cheerfulness and tangible expressions of affection.
81. Planning to spend some time alone with her for sharing and communicating every day.
82. Remembering to tell her when you must work late.
83. Refusing to work late on a regular basis.
84. Taking care of the yard work properly.
85. Helping the children with their homework.
86. Refusing to compare her unfavorably with other people.

87. Handling money wisely.
88. Not allowing work, church, or recreational activities to keep you from fulfilling marriage or family responsibilities.
89. Trying to find things to do with her.
90. Being willing to go out or stay home with her.
91. Being polite, courteous, and mannerly with her.
92. Refusing to be overly dependent on your parents or friends.
93. Developing mutual friends.
94. Providing adequate hospitalization insurance.
95. Trying to the level of your ability to provide housing and some support for your family in case you should die or become handicapped.
96. Being especially helpful and solicitous when she is not feeling well.
97. Being on time.
98. Going to P.T.A. with her.
99. Letting her sleep in once in a while by getting the children breakfast and, if possible, off to school.
100. Frequently giving in to her and allowing her to have her own way unless to do so would be sinful.
101. Putting children to bed at night.
102. Being gentle and tender and holding her before and after sexual relations.
103. Not nit-picking and finding fault, and giving the impression that you expect her to be perfect.

PLEASE LIST AND RECORD

"Let each of us please his neighbor for his good to his edification" (Rom. 15:2).

"Let nothing be done through selfishness or empty conceit but with humility of mind let each of you regard one another as more important than himself; do not merely look out for your own personal interests, but also for the interests of others" (Phil. 2:3, 4).

Pick several small areas of behavior where you really want to change to obey God and please your mate. Make sure the changes you want to make or things you want to do are:

1. Specific and not abstract or vague ("I want to be nice, or more loving" is too vague);
2. Attainable—be realistic;
3. Repeatable on a daily basis or at least frequently;
4. Positive and not merely negative—not merely, "I won't be critical," but, "I will express appreciation for at least two things every day";
5. Something which you may do and will do regardless of what the other person does or doesn't do.

Examples:

    I will smile when I enter the house;
    I will say I love you at least two times a day;
    I will call her from work to express my love;
    I will lead family devotions every day;
    I will plan my day so I can spend 30 minutes with her.

Name ———————————————

Put a check mark below the date when you performed your desired behavior.

Month and year ————————————————

Write out the
SPECIFIC BEHAVIOR   Date 1   2   3   4   5   6   7   8   9   10 11 12 13 14 15

SPECIFIC BEHAVIOR	Date				

Name _____

Put a check mark below the date when you performed your desired behavior.

Month and year _____

Write out the
SPECIFIC BEHAVIOR   Date 16 17 18 19 20 21 22 23 24 25 26 27 28 29 30 31

APPRECIATION AND ANNOYANCE LIST

Name _____ Date _____

THINGS YOU APPRECIATE ABOUT YOUR WIFE	WAYS TO SHOW APPRECIATION TO YOUR WIFE
1. _____	1. _____
2. _____	2. _____
3. _____	3. _____
4. _____	4. _____
5. _____	5. _____
6. _____	6. _____
7. _____	7. _____
8. _____	8. _____
9. _____	9. _____
10. _____	10. _____
11. _____	11. _____
12. _____	12. _____

Discuss your personal habits that annoy your wife. Begin to work on correcting them unless to do so would contradict the Bible.

1. _____

2. _____

3. _____

4. _____

5. _____

6. _____

7. _____

8. _____

9. _____

10. _____

HOW DO I RATE AS A LOVER?
(Husbands)

1. Do I really love my wife?
2. Read I Corinthians 13:1-8.
   a. Consider how I Corinthians 13:1-3 emphasizes the importance of love.
      vs. 1. *Love is more than beautiful words.*
      vs. 2. *Without love spiritual gifts and abilities are of little value.*
      vs. 3. *Extreme religious sacrifice without love is not pleasing to God.*
   b. Read I Corinthians 13:4-8 and note what love is, does, and doesn't do.
      Remember, Christ our Lord is the personification and perfect example of
      this kind of love. Remember also that this Bible passage was written to
      Christians, whose sins are forgiven and who are indwelt by the Holy Spirit.
      I Corinthians 13 describes the kind of love a Christian may have because of
      what God has done and is doing for and in him. On a separate sheet of
      paper record everything that I Corinthians 13:4-8 says about true love.
   c. On a scale of 0–4 rate how you score as your wife's lover on each of the
      15 aspects of love mentioned in I Corinthians 13:4-8. Try to recall and
      record at least one example of how you manifested or failed to manifest
      each of the 15 aspects.
   d. From this evaluation note especially how you need to improve as your
      wife's lover. Ask God and your wife for forgiveness and help, and go to
      work seeking to improve.

3. Am I actively serving, meeting needs, fulfilling legitimate desires, attempting
   to please and help my wife?
   a. Study Galatians 5:13-15; I John 3:16-18; Luke 6:27-38; Ephesians 5:
      25-28 and record the way love expresses itself to other people. Note also
      Philippians 2:1-4; Romans 13:8-10; 15:1, 2.
   b. List at least 15 ways you do or will love your wife in practical, tangible,
      unselfish, and perhaps sacrificial ways. Think especially in terms of her
      desires, likes and dislikes, requests and suggestions. Think in terms of
      the various aspects of your wife's life (physical, intellectual, spiritual,
      personal, financial, social, recreational, sexual, emotional, work, family,
      etc.), and plan how you may please or serve her in each of these areas.

Section Three

HOMEWORK

FOR WIVES

SAMPLE LOG LIST: WIFE AND MOTHER

Read Matthew 7:2-5; Romans 14:7-23; Ephesians 4:25-32; James 1:16; I John 1:9; Proverbs 28:13. As mentioned in the title, this list is merely suggestive. Go over it and personalize it where it fits your sins and faults. Add others to it as you examine your own life.

1. I seldom pray. My prayer life is very sporadic. When do you pray?
2. I don't enjoy reading the Bible as I used to. How much do you read?
3. I make excuses for not attending church. Why?
4. I resent the fact that we live where we do.
5. I demand too much of my husband's _____. What? How?
6. I am jealous and suspicious of _____. About what?
7. I am too critical of _____. About what?
8. I am bossy. With whom? About what?
9. I am too concerned with outward appearances. Examples?
10. I have bestowed too much time, money, attention to _____.
11. I'm not as happy as I pretend to be. I put on a false front. About what?
12. I'm much too worldly and carnal in my thinking, actions, and dress.
13. I'm too moody. About what? When? Examples.
14. I resent being tied down by the children or having no children.
15. I've been too insensitive to my husband's problems and concerns. Which?
16. I'm too concerned about money. How manifested?
17. I'm too much of a perfectionist in my housekeeping. How manifested?
18. I've not been willing to go camping or bowling or _____
    with _____ or to work on our cabin.
19. I've never liked his parents or his older brother.
20. I've tried to please my parents too much when I should have been more concerned about pleasing him. Examples.
21. I was more concerned about a new career in _____
    when motherhood should have been the most important thing to me.
22. I have not sufficiently appreciated what his parents have done for us.
23. I argue with him about _____ when I should be submissive. Examples?
24. I'm too outspoken at times when others are around. Examples?

25. I don't always pay attention when he is telling me something or explaining something to me. Examples?
26. I am a worry wart about _____.
27. I fret over the smallest things and blow them out of proportion. Examples?
28. My faith is very weak. How manifested?
29. I try to please others more than God. Examples?
30. I often allow my mind to wander during sermons and come away empty.
31. I've always been too apologetic about being a Christian. Examples?
32. I'm much too quick to condemn others. About what?
33. I haven't accepted my husband's role as leader and decision-maker as I should. How manifested?
34. I form my own opinions and try to carry out my own desires even when it hurts him. Examples?
35. I make decisions without first asking God for guidance. Examples?
36. I nag him about washing the car, mowing the yard, and fixing things around the house or _____.
37. Sometimes I forget to do things that he asks me to do. Examples?
38. Too often I allow his depression to rub off onto me, and then I'm not able to help and encourage him at all.
39. I try to be around him all the time and to always be doing things with him when I know he also needs time just to be alone.
40. I expect him to spend a lot of time in the evenings with the children, even when I know he is very, very tired.
41. I put the children's needs ahead of his. Examples?
42. I allow the baby's crying to make me irritable, etc.
43. I grumble about gathering up the trash so he can carry it out.
44. I complain about not eating out like we used to before the children came.
45. I sometimes feel depressed and unsatisfied with our sexual relations. When? Why? How aren't you satisfied?
46. I feel inferior to _____. About what?
47. I can often be negative and pessimistic in my outlook. Examples?
48. I complain about not having a second car instead of making the effort to take him to work so I can keep the car.
49. I often do not give him my enthusiastic support and cooperation in his role as the leader of the family. Examples?
50. I will not express affection as he wants me to. What won't you do?
51. I watch too much TV. I watch wrong programs.
52. I complain about not having any friends but I don't do anything about it.
53. I removed the wallpaper in the bedroom that _____ liked and haven't made any effort to put any more on the ugly wall though I

know he wants me to. (Or something like this.)

54. I often resort to self-pity. About what? When? Give examples.

55. I gossip about what _____ or _____
    has done.

56. I do not cooperate in the _____ activities of the church
    as I should. What should you do that you aren't doing?

57. I don't keep the beds made.

58. I begin to cry when he disagrees with me about the way we should spend our

    money or _____.

59. I often neglect the wash and ironing.

60. I make excuses for my laziness and failure to fulfill responsibilities. What
    responsibilities are you failing to fulfill?

61. I allow the children to disobey me until finally I get so disturbed that I
    begin to yell and scream at them. Examples?

62. I sometimes forget that _____ and I aren't on opposing
    teams, but on the same team. Specific examples of failure.

63. I become irritated with him about the way he spends money.

64. I forget to tell him about the phone messages for him.

65. When he comes home from work I complain and grumble about (the chil-

    dren, my aches and pains, etc.) _____.

66. I get irritated by his weaknesses instead of accepting him, praying for him,
    encouraging him, and setting an example for him. Give specific examples.

67. I am too quick to state my opinion to him and to belittle his opinion. Give
    specific examples.

68. I do not agree with the way he disciplines the children. Example? I let them
    get away with things that he would never approve of. Examples?

69. I often say I'm too tired to do what he wants me to do. Examples?

70. I am seldom ready at the time he wants to leave for some place. Examples?

71. When he comes home from work, I and the house often look like a disaster
    area. I am often so busy that I hardly have time for a peck on the cheek, let
    alone to sit down and talk with him, rub his back, or just to be close to him
    while drinking a cup of coffee.

72. When the children don't do their chores, I nag, criticize, complain, or yell.

73. I don't really listen to what my children have to say.

74. I don't take time to give each child personal attention.

75. I sometimes resent all the work that is involved in taking care of the chil-
    dren. What work do you resent?

76. I am more concerned about my children's physical and social well-being
    than about their spiritual well-being. How manifested?

77. I know that some things I do or don't do annoy _____
    but I am stubborn and won't change. Examples?
78. I make fun of him in front of the children and other people. Examples?
79. I do not manifest my love in tangible ways as he desires. In what ways?
80. I sometimes argue with him about his decisions in front of the children. Examples?
81. I do not cooperate with him in family devotions. In what ways?
82. I do not deal with issues or problems when they are beginning. Examples?
83. I keep a record of wrongs that people have done to me. I don't practice biblical forgiveness. Examples?
84. When he makes a wrong decision or fails, I call it to his attention. Sometimes I let him know that if he had listened to me he wouldn't have made the mistake. Examples?
85. I am inconsiderate of his desires. For example, he likes me to wear perfume, or rub his back, or go walking with him, but I think these things are unimportant. Examples?
86. I complain about the work he does for the church rather than cooperate and assist. Examples?
87. I don't like to go to the trouble of having people in for dinner.
88. I expect too much of him and the children and am hurt and disturbed when they don't perform as I want them to. Examples?
89. I make promises or threats to the children that I don't keep. Examples?

90. I overprotect the children by _____.
91. I fulfill the children's responsibilities instead of teaching them to fulfill their own responsibilities. Examples?
92. I don't take time to play with or just let the children know how much they mean to me.
93. I often refuse to have sexual relations with him and almost never ask him to have intercourse.
94. I allow my mother to meddle in our family. I often tell her things about him that make her think less of him. I am sometimes concerned more about pleasing my parents than about pleasing my husband. Examples?
95. I often make inordinate demands on him, expecting too much of him. Examples?
96. I blame things on him that are actually my fault. Examples?
97. I spend too much time away from home and am not available to him or the children frequently.
98. I try to push him into things. Give examples. I am not content until he has come around to my point of view or made the changes I want made or done what I want done.
99. I lose my temper frequently. About what? Note specifically what occasions your loss of temper.

100. I do not trust _____ as I should. About what?
101. I expect him to know what I want, to know my desires, ideas, concerns, to see things as I see them without even sharing my innermost feelings and opinions with him. When he doesn't, I think he doesn't care about me, and

then I become hurt and withdraw or _____.
Give examples.
102. I take things too seriously and often make mountains out of molehills. I sometimes major on minors. Give examples.
103. I sometimes flirt with other men to make him jealous or to get a good feeling (I am still attractive to men, I am still worthwhile, etc.).
104. I complain about his lack of decisiveness or silence or lack of initiative, but have become upset with him when he is decisive or aggressive or open in expressing his opinions. Give examples.
105. I refuse to ask him for advice about some things or talk over certain problems with him. Give examples.
106. I do not take care of myself physically as I should. Be specific.
107. I smoke too much.
108. I drink too much.
109. I use profanity. I take God's name in vain.
110. I have annoying habits and mannerisms. What are they?

111. _____

112. _____

113. _____

114. _____

SCORE CARD FOR WIVES

If you honestly evaluate yourself by this score card, you will be able to discern where you are failing and where you need to improve to be the helper God wants you to be to your husband. Suggestion—if you really want to know how you are doing, ask your husband to rate you.

Rating scale: never = 0; seldom = 1; sometimes = 2; frequently = 3; almost always = 4.

1. Do you try to make your home interesting, attractive, cheerful, a place of rest and relaxation—devoting as much thought and study to it as you would to a job downtown? ____

2. Do you serve meals that are enticing in variety and attractiveness? ____

3. Do you handle the finances that are your responsibility in a business-like fashion? ____

4. Do you keep yourself attractive in appearance in order that your husband may be glad to have everyone know you are his wife? ____

5. Are you a good sport, cheerful, uncomplaining, appreciative, and not a nag? ____

6. Are you willing to let your husband have his own way and the last word when you disagree? ____

7. Do you avoid making a fuss over trifles and solve minor problems that you should handle alone? ____

8. Do you show respect and admiration for him, not comparing him unfavorably with other men, but making him think that you esteem him above all other men? ____

9. Do you prevent your mother and other relatives from intruding unduly and show courtesy and consideration to his relatives? ____

10. Do you take a sympathetic and intelligent interest in his business, yet leave him a free hand, realizing that he must sometimes give time to his business that you would rather have him give to you? ____

11. Do you cultivate an interest in his friends and recreations, so you can make a satisfactory partner of his leisure hours? ____

12. Do you pray regularly with and for your husband and maintain a good devotional life? ____

13. Do you seek his counsel on important decisions? ____

14. Do you support his decisions and cheerfully assist him in fulfilling them? ____

15. Do you show respect and esteem for him with the children and other people? ____

16. Do you lovingly share your ideas, problems, joys, interests, and affection with him on a regular basis? ____

17. Do you enthusiastically and unselfishly seek to satisfy his sexual desires? ____

HOUSE CLEANING

Mrs. Carol Mack

A. General Rules
1. Keep the house "decent and in order."*
2. Do the things that matter most to your husband.

Test for me: Am I embarrassed when the doorbell rings and I'm not expecting anyone?

B. Specific Suggestions
1. Do everything *once* every week—floors, dusting, bathrooms, etc.
2. Do things more than once if necessary to fulfill nos. 1 and 2 above.
3. Every week do two things that don't get done on a weekly basis; e.g., straightening up closets, windows, kitchen cabinets.
4. Every week do one or two rooms "extra good."
5. In order to fulfill nos. 1 and 2, do a lot of "straightening up" every morning.
6. Plan a time every weekday when you will clean. Do one or two rooms every weekday. Plan which rooms you will do on certain days.
7. Plan your work and work your plan!

C. Weekly Check Up List

	Monday	Tuesday	Wednesday	Thursday	Friday
Kitchen floor					
Counters					
Bathrooms					
Toilets					
Woodwork					
Windows					
Laundry					
Living room					
Dining room					
Den					
Family room					
Bedroom #1					
Bedroom #2					
Bedroom #3					
Bedroom #4					

* Everything depends on what you mean by "decent and in order." If you think you are getting careless, start having people in for dinner, coffee, friends for lunch, etc.

WAYS A WIFE MAY EXPRESS LOVE TO HER HUSBAND
(How to Convince Your Husband That You Love Him)

Evaluate the way you express love to your husband. Go over the list and circle the ways you are neglecting. Ask your husband to go over the list and put a check mark in front of the ways he would like you to express love. Ask him to add other things to the list.

You may express love to your husband by:

1. Greeting him at the door when he comes home with a smile, a hug, a kiss, and an, "Am I glad to see you. I really missed you today."
2. Having a cup of coffee or tea ready for him when he comes home.
3. Giving him a lingering kiss.
4. Letting him know you like to be with him and making arrangements so that you can spend time with him without giving the impression that you really should or would rather be doing something else.
5. Being willing to talk to him about his concerns and not belittling him for having these concerns.
6. Supporting him and cooperating with him enthusiastically and positively when he has made a decision.
7. Teasing and flirting with him.
8. Seeking to arouse him and sometimes being the aggressor or leader in sex relations.
9. Asking him to have sex relations more than he would expect you to.
10. Really letting yourself go when having sexual relations.
11. Caressing him.
12. Looking at him with an adoring expression.
13. Sitting close to him.
14. Holding his hand.
15. Rubbing his back or. . . .
16. Wearing his favorite nightgown or dress or perfume or. . . .
17. Expressing your love in words or notes.
18. Letting him know how much you appreciate him and what you appreciate about him. Do this often and for things that are sometimes taken for granted. Pretend you are trying to convince him you think he is great and very important to you.
19. Frequently fulfilling his wishes and desires as well as the specific requests he makes of you. Try to anticipate what he might desire or wish and surprise him by doing it before he asks.
20. Playing with him (tennis, golf, party games, etc.); sharing his hobbies and interests.

21. Enthusiastically cooperating with him and sharing with him in devotions and prayer; seeking to set a good example to the children concerning their attitude toward devotions and prayer.
22. Maintaining your own spiritual life through regular Bible study and prayer.
23. Handling your affairs decently and in order; structuring your time and using it wisely.
24. Being willing to face and solve problems even if it requires discomfort, change, and much effort.
25. Fulfilling your responsibilities.
26. Asking him for his advice and frequently following it.
27. Being ready to leave at the appointed time.
28. Standing with him and supporting him in his attempts to raise your children for God.
29. Thanking him in creative ways for his attempts to please you.
30. Asking for forgiveness and saying, "I was wrong and will try to change."
31. Actually changing where you should.
32. Working with him on his projects or. . . .
33. Reading the literature he asks you to read and sharing your insights.
34. Letting him know when he has tough decisions to make (and even when they are not so tough) that you really believe he will choose the right thing and that you will wholeheartedly support him in whatever decision he makes, provided the decision does not violate clearly revealed biblical principle; being his best cheerleader and fan club.
35. Buying gifts for him.
36. Watching football or other sporting events with him and trying to really manifest an interest.
37. Keeping the house neat and clean.
38. Cooking creatively and faithfully.
39. Having devotions with the children when he is not able to be there.
40. Maintaining his disciplinary rules when he is not present.
41. Being appreciative and cooperative when he holds you, caresses or kisses you.
42. Lovingly giving him your input when you think he is in error.
43. Offering constructive suggestions when you think he could improve or become more productive. Don't push or preach or do this in such a way that you belittle him, but seek positive and non-threatening ways to help him become more fully the man God wants him to be.
44. Running errands gladly.
45. Seeking to complete, not compete with, him; being the best member of his team and seeking to convince him that you are just that.
46. Being lovingly honest with him—no back door messages—no withholding of truth that will hinder your relationship or future trust and closeness.
47. Being willing to see things from his point of view; putting the best interpreta-

tion on what he does or says until you have evidence that proves the contrary.
48. Pampering him and making a fuss over him.
49. Being happy and cheerful.
50. Refusing to nag.
51. Gently brushing a leg under the table.
52. Having candlelight and music at dinner.
53. Indicating you want to be alone with him and talk or just lie in each other's arms.
54. Giving an "I promise you" wink.
55. Going for a walk with him.
56. Letting him know you feel lonely when he is out of town or away from you for a period of time.
57. Relating what happened to you during your day.
58. Sharing your fears, concerns, joys, failures, etc.
59. Seeking to support your ideas with biblical insights and good reasons.
60. Refusing to "cop out" or withdraw and attack or exaggerate or blameshift when he seeks to make constructive suggestions or discuss problems.
61. Giving him your undivided attention when he wants to talk.
62. Discussing the meaning of certain Bible passages or discussing how to improve your marriage or home or children or child raising efforts, etc.
63. Cheerfully staying up past your bedtime to resolve a disagreement or problem.
64. Holding him close while expressing genuine concern and tangible and vocal love when he is hurt, discouraged, weary, or burdened.
65. Being eager to share a good joke or some other interesting information you have learned.
66. Working in the yard or painting a room together or washing the car.
67. Planning vacations or trips together.
68. Wanting to keep your family memorabilia, newspaper clippings, church releases, etc., that have to do with your family.
69. Bragging to others about him and his accomplishments and how good a husband he is.
70. Joining with him in a team ministry at the church.
71. Doing a Bible study or Bible research together.
72. Doing a good job in bookkeeping about family finances.
73. Helping prepare the income tax report.
74. Keeping touch through letters with your family and friends.
75. Keeping yourself attractive and clean.
76. Inviting other people in for dinner or fellowship.
77. Developing and using the spiritual gifts God has given you.
78. Asking him to pray with you about something.
79. Expressing how much you love the children and being the children's cheerleader.

80. Managing to stay within the family budget and even saving some for special surprises.
81. Being excited about sharing the gospel with others or about answered prayer or about helping other people.
82. Making a list for him of things that need to be done around the house.
83. Being satisfied with your present standard of living or furniture or equipment when he can provide no more.
84. Not making nostalgic comments about your father's way of providing, etc., which may seem to imply that you think your father was a much better man than your husband.
85. Acknowledging that there are some specific areas or ways in which you need to improve.
86. Taking care of his clothes so that he is always dressed well.
87. Appreciating and helping his mother and father and relatives.
88. Refusing to disagree with him in the presence of others.
89. Cooperating with him in establishing family goals and procedures and then in fulfilling them.
90. Being silly and unconventional in your lovemaking at times.
91. Telling him before he asks you that you think he has done a good job, if he has done a good job. Don't be afraid of repeating yourself in commending him for what he is or does.
92. Being available and eager to fulfill his desires wherever and whenever it is proper and possible.
93. Beginning each day with cheerfulness and tangible expressions of affection.
94. Letting the children know that you and your husband are in agreement; communicating to your children when your husband can hear (and when he cannot) how wonderful he is.

PLEASE LIST AND RECORD

"Let each of us please his neighbor for his good to his edification" (Rom. 15:2).

"Let nothing be done through selfishness or empty conceit but with humility of mind let each of you regard one another as more important than himself; do not merely look out for your own personal interests, but also for the interests of others" (Phil. 2:3, 4).

Pick several small areas of behavior where you really want to change to obey God and please your mate. Make sure the changes you want to make or things you want to do are:

1. Specific and not abstract or vague ("I want to be nice, or more loving" is too vague);

2. Attainable—be realistic;

3. Repeatable on a daily basis or at least frequently;

4. Positive and not merely negative—not merely "I won't be critical," but, "I will express appreciation for at least two things every day."

5. Something which you may and will do regardless of what the other person does or doesn't do.

Examples:

I will smile when he enters the house;
I will say I love you at least two times a day;
I will put on perfume and dress neatly when he arrives home after work;
I will cooperate in family devotions every day;
I will plan my day so I can spend 30 minutes with him.

Name ——————————————————

Put a check mark below the date when you performed your desired behavior.

Month and year ——————————————————

Write out the
SPECIFIC BEHAVIOR   Date 1   2   3   4   5   6   7   8   9   10 11 12 13 14 15

Name _____

Put a check mark below the date when you performed your desired behavior.

Month and year _____

Write out the
SPECIFIC BEHAVIOR   Date 16 17 18 19 20 21 22 23 24 25 26 27 28 29 30 31

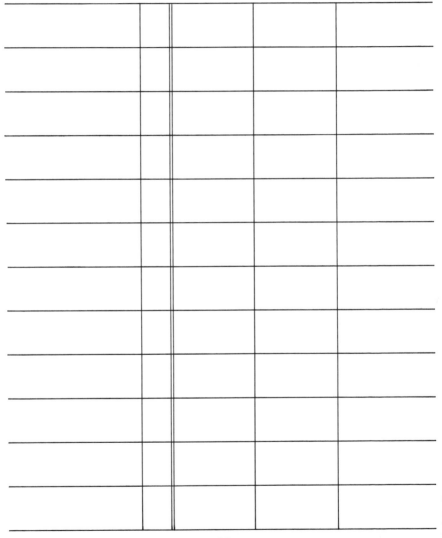

APPRECIATION AND ANNOYANCE LIST

Name _____ Date _____

THINGS YOU APPRECIATE ABOUT YOUR HUSBAND	WAYS TO SHOW APPRECIATION TO YOUR HUSBAND
1. _____	1. _____
2. _____	2. _____
3. _____	3. _____
4. _____	4. _____
5. _____	5. _____
6. _____	6. _____
7. _____	7. _____
8. _____	8. _____
9. _____	9. _____
10. _____	10. _____
11. _____	11. _____
12. _____	12. _____

Discuss your personal habits that annoy your husband. Begin to work on correcting them unless to do so would contradict the Bible.

1. _____
2. _____
3. _____
4. _____
5. _____
6. _____
7. _____
8. _____
9. _____
10. _____

HOW DO I RATE AS A LOVER?
(Wives)

1. Do I really love my husband?

2. Read I Corinthians 13:1-8.
   a. Consider how I Corinthians 13:1-3 emphasizes the importance of love.
      vs. 1. *Love is more than beautiful words.*
      vs. 2. *Without love spiritual gifts and abilities are of little value.*
      vs. 3. *Extreme religious sacrifice without love is not pleasing to God.*
   b. Read I Corinthians 13:4-8 and note what love is, does, and doesn't do. Remember, Christ our Lord is the personification and perfect example of this kind of love. Remember also that this Bible passage was written to Christians, whose sins are forgiven and who are indwelt by the Holy Spirit. I Corinthians 13 describes the kind of love a Christian may have because of what God has done and is doing for and in him. On a separate sheet of paper record everything that I Corinthians 13:4-8 says about true love.
   c. On a scale of 0–4 rate how you score as your husband's lover on each of the 15 aspects of love mentioned in I Corinthians 13:4-8. Try to recall and record at least one example of how you manifested or failed to manifest each of the 15 aspects.
   d. From this evaluation note especially how you need to improve as your husband's lover. Ask God and your husband for forgiveness and help, and go to work seeking to improve.

3. Am I actively serving, meeting needs, fulfilling legitimate desires, attempting to please and help my husband?
   a. Study Galatians 5:13-15; I John 3:16-18; Luke 6:27-38; Ephesians 5:25-28 and record the way love expresses itself to other people. Note also Philippians 2:1-4; Romans 13:8-10; 15:1, 2.
   b. List at least 15 ways you do or will love your husband in practical, tangible, unselfish, and perhaps sacrificial ways. Think especially in terms of his desires, likes and dislikes, requests and suggestions. Think in terms of the various aspects of your husband's life (physical, intellectual, spiritual, personal, financial, social, recreation, sexual, emotional, work, family, etc.), and plan how you may please or serve him in each of these areas.

Section Four

HOMEWORK

FOR PARENTS

AND CHILDREN

HOW TO AVOID PROVOKING CHILDREN TO WRATH

Ephesians 6:4

I

THE PRIMARY RESPONSIBILITY BELONGS TO FATHERS

A. Mothers are involved (Ex. 20:12; Prov. 1:8, 9; 6:20; 20:20; I Tim. 5:10; II Tim. 3:15; Eph. 6:1-3).

B. Fathers are prone to neglect the biblical doctrine of the headship of husbands (e.g., Eli—I Sam. 2:12, 22-25; 3:11-13).

C. I Timothy 3:4, 5: As manager of his family, a responsible father:
   1. Knows family members;
   2. Has goals and plans;
   3. Delegates and motivates;
   4. Knows how to get along with people (social skills);
   5. Shows foresight—school, puberty, peer pressure, dating, sexual desires, decisions, marriage, occupation (Rom. 12:17; Luke 14:28-33);
   6. Is approachable (I Cor. 13:4-8; I Tim. 3:2, 3);
   7. Is available, accessible (I Pet. 5:1; Deut. 6:7).

II

DON'T PROVOKE CHILDREN TO WRATH

A. *This does not mean* never oppose, deny, or cross children, or do anything that might precipitate anger and displeasure in a child (I Sam. 3:11-13; Prov. 22:15; Heb. 12:5-11).

B. *It does mean* avoid doing those things that would tend to stimulate our children to a wrathful kind of living.
   1. Hodge: Parents "are not to excite the bad passions of their children," nor is a father "by *his own ill conduct* [to] nurture evil in the heart of his child."
   2. Hendriksen: "Do not exasperate or embitter your children"; "Do not provoke your children to an *angry mood.*"
   3. In other words, do not provoke your children to a wrathful kind of living, to become angry young men or women.
      a. A man given to anger (Prov. 22:24).
      b. A man of great anger (Prov. 19:19).
      c. A man who has no control over his spirit (Prov. 25:28).

C. The Bible describes at least two kinds of anger (I Sam. 15:23):
   1. *Open rebellion,* hostility, exploding, blowing up, displaying a hot temper (Prov. 14:29; 15:18; 19:19; 22:24; 29:11).

a. Against God;

b. Against parents;

c. Against authority;

d. Against anyone who opposes;

e. Against anyone and almost everyone.

2. *Passive resentment,* apathy, indifference, withdrawal, silence, suicidal inclinations, sub par performance. This anger is *bottled,* held down and in (Eph. 4:26, 27, 31; Col. 3:21).

D. *How might parents provoke children to wrath?*

1. *Neglect or ignore them* (Deut. 6:7, 8; Prov. 5:16, 17; 27:8; I Sam. 2:22; II Sam. 14:28-29).

2. *Abuse them physically,* e.g., by punching, kicking, slapping, shaking, throwing, beating, shoving, etc. (Exod. 20:13; I Cor. 13:4-8; James 1:19, 20).

3. *Abuse them psychologically,* e.g., by such words as clumsy, no good, stupid, sloppy, dummy; by actions; by expressions; by tone of voice (Eph. 4:29; Prov. 15:1; 16:21, 23, 24; Col. 4:6).

4. *Constantly find fault with them* (Prov. 11:9, 11; 12:6, 18; 16:27).

a. "How come you . . . ?"

b. "You missed. . . ."

c. "You didn't. . . ."

d. "You forgot. . . ."

5. *Refuse to listen to them* (Prov. 18:2, 13, 15; James 1:19).

a. Sending off "busy signals."

b. Allowing no input, discussion, explanations, or questions.

6. *Be too permissive* (I Kings 1:5, 6; Prov. 29:15b). "I don't want my child to be inhibited." "I don't want to destroy creativity."

7. *Demand too much of them* intellectually, spiritually, physically, emotionally (Gen. 33:13; Prov. 22:6; I Cor. 13:11).

8. *Have double standards or changing standards.*

a. Parent vs. children.

b. Wrong today, right tomorrow, wrong the next day, depending on the energy or mood of parent (Matt. 7:1-5; Rom. 2:1-3).

9. *Have constant marital or parental discord or conflict. Many* behavioral or attitudinal problems are *often* a *reflection* of three things:

a. Personal problems in parents (Prov. 13:20; 22:24, 25).

b. Marital problems—difficulties between husband and wife.

c. Failure to follow the biblical directives for parenting (Prov. 11:29).

WORKSHEET FOR PARENTS — NO. I

*1. How would you describe your relationship with each of your children? List the name of each child and then describe your relationship as excellent (5), very good (4), good (3), fair (2), poor (1), terrible (0). (If your children are very young, answer the questions with asterisks (*) as you imagine you would answer them if your children were older and you were facing the situations described in the questions.)

*2. If you rated your relationship with your child or children as excellent (5), very good (4), or good (3), jot down:
   a. your reasons for thinking you have a good relationship;
   b. what has hindered a better relationship;
   c. what you must now do to improve your relationship.

3. Put yourself in the place of your children and imagine what you would want from a parent if you were they. What would you want a parent to be? to provide for you? to do for you? Make a list of specific things and then ask if their expectations and desires are reasonable or unreasonable. Are there ways in which you could change without compromising biblical principle to become more the parent your children desire? Circle the ways you could change or improve.

4. List the name of each child and then write down everything you appreciate about each of them. Continue to add to this list. Make it a practice to look for the good qualities, actions, responses, attitudes, conduct, potential in each child. Communicate your appreciation regularly, specifically, and enthusiastically.

5. Make a list of at least 10 fun things that each child enjoys that you can do with him/her. Plan when you will do at least one of these things with your child (children) at least once a week. List all the fun things you did with your child (children) during the last month.

6. How would you describe the communication level of your family? (5) excellent, (4) very good, (3) good, (2) fair, (1) poor, (0) terrible.

7. What are the hindrances to communication on a family level? List them.

8. Is there any person in your family with whom you have the most difficulty communicating? What can you do to break through the communication barrier? How can you improve the communication level of your family?

9. List at least 15 ways that you do or can show love to your children. Think especially in terms of your children's desires, likes, and dislikes. Think in terms of the various aspects of their lives.

HOW TO RAISE A CHILD FOR GOD

Study the following principles and circle the ones where you are failing.

1. Examine your expectations for your child. Are they realistic? Evaluate them in the light of the Bible (I Cor. 13:11; Matt. 18:10; Gen. 33:12-14).

2. Love him unconditionally (Deut. 7:7; I John 4:10, 19).

3. Look for opportunities in which you can commend him. Express appreciation for him frequently (Phil. 1:3; I Thess. 1:2; II Thess. 1:3).

4. Seldom criticize without first expressing appreciation for good points (I Cor. 1:3-13).

5. Give him freedom to make decisions where serious issues are not at stake. Your goal should be to bring your child to maturity in Christ and not to dependence on you (Eph. 4:13-15; 6:4; Prov. 22:6; Col. 1:27, 28).

6. Do not compare him with others (Gal. 6:4; II Cor. 10:12, 13; I Cor. 12:4-11).

7. Never mock him or make fun of him. Do not demean or belittle your child. Beware of calling him dumb or clumsy or stupid (Matt. 7:12; Eph. 4:29, 30; Col. 4:6; Prov. 12:18; 16:24).

8. Do not scold him in front of others (Matt. 16:22, 23; 18:15; I Cor. 16:14).

9. Never make threats or promises that you do not intend to keep (Matt. 5:37; James 5:12; Col. 3:9).

10. Don't be afraid to say "no," and when you say it, mean it (Prov. 22:15; 29:15; I Sam. 3:13; Gen. 18:19).

11. When your child has problems or is a problem, do not overreact or lose control of yourself. Do not yell or shout or scream at him (Eph. 4:26, 27; I Cor. 16:14; II Tim. 2:24, 25; I Tim. 5:1, 2).

12. Communicate optimism and expectancy. Do not communicate by word or action that you have given up on your child and are resigned to his being a failure (Philem. 21; II Cor. 9:1, 2; I Cor. 13:7).

13. Make sure your child knows exactly what is expected of him. Most of the book of Proverbs is specific counsel from a father to his son.

14. Ask his advice—include him in some of the family planning (Rom. 1:11, 12; II Tim. 4:11; I Tim. 4:12; John 6:5).

15. When you make a mistake with your child, admit it and ask your child for forgiveness (Matt. 5:23, 24; James 5:16).

16. Have family conferences where you discuss:
    a. Family goals
    b. Family projects
    c. Vacations
    d. Devotions

e. Chores

f. Discipline

g. Complaints

h. Suggestions

i. Problems

Welcome contributions from your child (Ps. 128; James 1:19; 3:13-18; Titus 1:6-8; Prov. 15:22).

17. Assess his areas of strength and then encourage him to develop them. Begin with one and encourage him to really develop in this area (II Tim. 1:16; 4:5; I Pet. 4:10).

18. Give him plenty of tender loving care. Be free in your expression of love by word and deed (I Cor. 13:1-8; 16:14; John 13:34; I Thess. 2:7, 8).

19. Practice selective reinforcement. When your child does something well, commend him. Especially let him know when his attitude and effort are what they should be (I Thess. 1:3-10; Phil. 1:3-5; Col. 1:3, 4; Eph. 1:15).

20. Be more concerned about Christian attitudes and character than you are about performance or athletic skills or clothing or external beauty or intelligence (I Sam. 16:7; Gal. 5:22, 23; I Pet. 3:4, 5; Prov. 4:23; Matt. 23:25-28).

21. Have a lot of fun with your child. Plan to have many fun times and many special events with your child. Make a list of fun things your family can do (Ps. 128; Prov. 5:15-18; 15:13; 17:22; Eph. 6:4; Col. 3:21; Eccles. 3:4; Luke 15:22-24).

22. Help your child to learn responsibility by administering discipline fairly, consistently, lovingly, and promptly (I Sam. 3:13; Prov. 13:24; 19:18; 22:15).

23. Look upon your child as a human *becoming* as well as a human *being*. Look upon the task of raising children as a process which takes 18 to 19 years to complete (Eph. 6:4; Prov. 22:6; Gal. 6:9; I Cor. 15:58; Isa. 28:9, 10).

24. Live your convictions consistently. Your child will learn more by observing your example than he will by listening to your words (Deut. 6:4-9; I Thess. 2:10-12; Phil. 4:9; II Tim. 1:5, 7).

25. Recognize that you are responsible to prepare your child for life in this world and in the world to come (Eph. 6:4; Deut. 6:4-9; Ps. 78:5-7; II Tim. 3:15-17).

26. Be very sensitive to the needs, feelings, fears, and opinions of your child (Matt. 18:10; Col. 3:21).

27. Treat the child as though he is important to you and accepted by you (Matt. 18:5-6).

28. Avoid the use of words expressing anger or exasperation (Prov. 15:1; Eph. 4:31, 32).

29. Maintain the practice of daily Bible reading, discussions, and prayer (Deut. 6:4-9; II Tim. 3:15; Eph. 6:4; Ps. 1:1-3; 78:5-8; 119:9, 11).

30. Become thoroughly involved as a family in a biblical church (Heb. 10:24, 25; Eph. 4:11-16).

31. Make your home a center of Christian hospitality, where your child will be brought into frequent contact with many Christians (Rom. 12:13; Heb. 13: 1, 2; II Kings 4:8-37).

32. Make it easy for your child to approach you with problems, difficulties, and concerns. Learn to be a good listener when he needs you. Give your child your undivided attention. Avoid being a mind reader or an interrupter or a critic. Show an interest in whatever interests your child. Make yourself available when your child needs you—even if you are busy (James 1:19, 20; 3:16-18; I John 3:16-18; I Cor. 9:19-23; Phil. 2:3, 4).

33. Seek to bring your child to a saving knowledge of Jesus Christ. Become all things to your child that you might win your child to Christ. God, of course, must do the saving, bring conviction, give repentance and faith. You, however, may provide the environment in which God saves—by your prayers, godly speech and example, family devotions, and involvement in a sound biblical church (II Tim. 1:5-7; 3:14-17; Eph. 6:4; Deut. 6:4-9; Mark 10: 13, 14; Rom. 10:13-17; I Cor. 1:18-21).

GOD'S WAY OF BRINGING UP CHILDREN

Ephesians 6:4

I

BRING OUR CHILDREN UP

A. The verb is in the *active voice*. Greek has three voices: active, middle, passive.
   1. If middle, it would read, *Bring yourselves up.*
   2. If passive, it would read, *Be brought up.*
B. The verb is in the *present tense.*
C. The verb is in the *imperative mood.*
D. Note what the clause says we are to do: *bring them up.*
   1. Goal—not negative
   2. Goal—not dependence
   3. Goal—positive and spiritual
      a. Matthew 28:19
      b. Colossians 1:28
      c. Hebrews 5:13

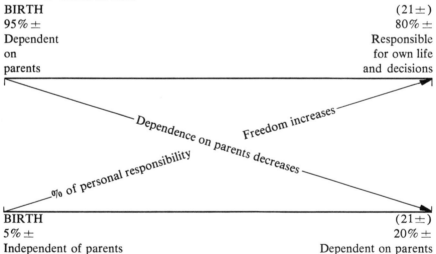

BIRTH (21±)
95%± 80%±
Dependent Responsible
on for own life
parents and decisions

Dependence on parents decreases / *Freedom increases*

% of personal responsibility

BIRTH (21±)
5%± 20%±
Independent of parents Dependent on parents

II

BRING UP IN THE "PAIDEIA" AND "NOUTHESIA" OF THE LORD

This involves three things:

A. *"Paideia"* = *instruction* (Titus 2:12; Acts 7:22; II Tim. 3:16; Prov. 5:12).
  1. What do we teach?
     a. Teach doctrine (II Tim. 3:15, 16).
     b. Teach proper standards and values.
        1) *World's* vs. 2) *God's* (Jer. 9:23, 24).
     c. Teach how to know God and have fellowship with Him (Ps. 27; Phil. 3).
     d. Teach how to be good stewards of:
        1) Talents (Rom. 12:3-8).
        2) Treasures (I Tim. 6:17, 18).
        3) Time (Eph. 5:16).
     e. Teach them to love and serve others (Luke 10:25-39; Phil. 2:3-11).
     f. Teach them to make decisions and live biblically—not on the basis of feelings (Ps. 119:105; Prov. 15:22; 16:3).
     g. Teach them the importance of discipline, integrity, honesty, dependability, and truthfulness (Christian character and conduct).
     h. Teach them how to solve their problems biblically (I Cor. 10:13; Matt. 7; 18).
     i. Teach them to respect God-ordained authority (Rom. 13; Heb. 13; Eph. 6).
     j. Teach them how to respond to hardship and mistreatment (Rom. 12).
     k. Teach them how to be good husbands and wives and parents (Eph. 4–6; I Cor. 7; 13; Prov. 31; I Pet. 3).
        1) How to be a good mate.
        2) How to choose a mate.
  2. How do we do it?
     a. Deuteronomy 6:4-25.
        1) *Personally experience the power of God's Word* (vss. 4-6).
        2) *Persistently explain the precepts of God's Word* (vss. 7, 20-25).
           a) Formal, structured.
           b) Informal, spontaneous.
        3) *Plainly exhibit the practicality of God's Word* (vss. 8, 9).
           a) Activities and attitudes.
           b) Private and public life.
     b. I Thessalonians 2:10-12: additional insights.
        1) *Exhorting*—calling to one's side to help.
        2) *Encouraging*—comforting.
        3) *Expediting*—imploring, urging, motivating.
        4) *Exhibiting*—verse 10.
B. *"Nouthesia"* = *counsel, admonition, warning* (Titus 3:10; I Cor. 10:11; Acts 20:31; Col. 3:16; Rom. 15:14).
  1. *Implies the existence of a problem* (Col. 1:28; I Thess. 5:14).
     a. Know what problems are.

b. Deal with them (Gal. 6:1).

2. *Involves isolating the problem by the use of appropriate questions.*
   a. What? (Eph. 4:29; James 4:11; 5:9).
   b. When? (Prov. 15:23; 25:11; 27:14).
   c. How? (Prov. 15:1; II Tim. 2:24, 25; Col. 4:6).
   d. Where? (Prov. 15:28; 29:20).
   e. To whom? (Matt. 18:15).
   f. How often? (Prov. 17:9; 10:19).
   g. Why? (Col. 3:8; Eph. 4:29).

3. *Implies attempting to correct with a spirit of genuine compassion and concern.*
   a. Acts 20:31.
   b. I Corinthians 4:14.
   c. Ephesians 4:15.

C. *"Paideia" = discipline, training* (Heb. 12:8, 11).
   1. What kind of discipline?
      a. The kind of discipline God uses with His children (Heb. 12:5-12; Gen. 2; 3; I Sam. 2; 3; I Cor. 11:30-32).
      b. The kind of discipline God prescribes in His Word (Prov. 13:24; 19:18; 22:6, 15; 23:13, 14; 29:15).
   2. How do we do it?
      a. *Establishing rules and regulations*
         1) For the good of our children (Deut. 5:29-33).
         2) Based upon biblical principles (I Sam. 8:20; Ps. 119:105, 128).
      b. *Explaining (discussing, clarifying)*
         1) God's example (Gen. 2; Exod. 20; etc.).
         2) Book of Proverbs.
      c. *Enforcing.*
         1) Modeling (I Thess. 1:5, 6; Phil. 4:9).
         2) Training (Heb. 5:14; I Tim. 4:7).
         3) Make obedience attractive—*motivate* (I Thess. 2:11, 12).
         4) Administer discipline—chastisement when rules are broken (Heb. 12:5-12; Prov. 13:24).
   3. Forms of corrective discipline: Be creative. God does not always use the same form (I Sam. 10:5; 11:4; Lam. 3:1; I Cor. 4:21. "Rod" is both figurative and literal).
      a. *Natural consequences* (Ps. 7:14-16; Luke 15:11-24).
      b. *Logical consequences* (II Thess. 3:10; Exod. 22:1; Deut. 31:16, 17).
      c. *Corporal punishment.*
         1) Proverbs 13:24; 22:15; 23:13, 14; 29:15.

2) Used when child is deliberately defiant or disobedient.
   a) Consistently.
   b) Corporately.
   c) Immediately.
   d) Sufficiently.
   e) Intelligently—with instruction.
   f) Prayerfully.
   g) Lovingly (Prov. 13:24; Heb. 12:5, 6).
   h) Under control (James 1:19, 20).
   i) Conclusively.

WORKSHEET FOR PARENTS — NO. 2

1. Consider your parental goals. What qualities do you want to see developed in your children? By the time they are 21 or 22, what kind of persons would you like them to be? What do you hope will have been accomplished? What do you desire they will be prepared to be or do?

2. Compare your goals with the goals that God has for His children. Study the following verses and notice what God wants His children to become. Certainly our goals and His goals should coincide (Matt. 28:19, 20; Exod. 20:1-17; Matt. 22:36-40; Eph. 4:1–6:20; Rom. 12:1–15:7; I Cor. 13; Phil. 2:1-18; 4:1-9; Matt. 5:1–7:27; Luke 6:27-49; Gal. 5:13–6:10).

3. Discuss and write down how you will attempt to assist your children to become and do everything that God wants them to be and do. (Study Phil. 4:9; II Tim. 1:5; 3:15-17; Deut. 6:4-9; Heb. 12:5-11; Prov. 3:11, 12; 1:8, 9; 22:6, 15, 24, 25; 13:20, 24; 29:15; Eph. 6:4; I Tim. 4:16; 5:8; I Cor. 15:33; Gal. 6:7, 8.)

4. Examine the kind of discipline you are giving to your children. Discuss and write down your answers to the following questions:

   a. What are your children's chores and responsibilities? Do you know? Do they?

   b. What are your disciplinary rules and procedures? Do you know what you expect in specific terms? Do they? Children must know clearly what is expected of them and what will happen if they obey or disobey. Are your expectations realistic and rewards and correction appropriate?

   c. Do you administer discipline consistently and sufficiently?

   d. Do you administer discipline fairly with instruction and love?

   e. Do you impart the idea that you expect obedience and put the prescribed discipline into effect when the child does not immediately obey?

   f. Do you and your mate agree on your expectations and the mechanics of discipline? Don't expect your children to obey or agree or respond to your discipline if you and your mate do not support each other.

   g. Do you really make obedience attractive? Do you think of discipline positively or merely negatively?

5. Study Deuteronomy 6:4-9.

   a. List the parental responsibilities mentioned in this passage.

   b. Discuss how you are fulfilling the parental responsibilities mentioned here. What else could you do?

81

6. Examine what you are teaching your children about the following areas or subjects by your example:
   a. Loyalty and devotion to God.
   b. Sex
   c. Work
   d. Money
   e. Time
   f. Marriage
   g. How to treat parents
   h. Being a neighbor
   i. Spiritual mindedness
   j. Honesty and truthfulness
   k. What is really important in life
   l. Self-control
   m. Church attendance and involvement
   n. Respect and concern for other people
   o. How to face and solve problems
   p. How to react to criticism
   q. Bible reading and study
   r. Decision making
   s. Prayer
   t. Others _____ _____

7. Select areas in which you should become a better example. Ask God for help and go to work.

BEHAVIOR CONTRACT

RULE	*Desired Behavior*	REWARD	PUNISHMENT
I.	Chores Rooms cleaned Dishes Trash Lawn mowed	Personal satisfaction, training for life, commendation by parents, acceptable TV programs	Denial of privileges until work completed, extra work
II.	General obedience	Personal satisfaction, no rod, harmony and unity and happiness in home	Rod, privileges denied
III.	Cooperation with respect and concern for other people	Personal satisfaction, training for life, usefulness, friends, happiness, help from others	Isolation, essays, guilt, enemies, bad patterns, privileges denied
IV.	Truthfulness honesty integrity industry dependability		
V.	School work done well		
VI.	Cooperation and cheerful participation in family projects, family devotions and church activities		

BEHAVIOR CONTRACT

RULE	REWARD	PUNISHMENT
I.		
II.		
III.		
IV.		
V.		
VI.		

DAILY CHECKUP CHART

FOR _____

Week of _____

When you have completed the *task* or *activity* listed at the left, put a check mark in the appropriate column at the right.

                                Mon. Tues. Wed. Thurs. Fri. Sat.

1. Made bed _____

2. Cleaned up room _____

3. Shared day with family _____

4. Bible reading and prayer _____

5. _____

6. _____

7. _____

8. _____

9. _____

10. _____

11. _____

12. _____

13. _____

14. _____

BIBLE STUDY ON FAMILY RELIGION

A. Describe what the following verses have to say about family religion.

1. Genesis 18:19: _____

2. Exodus 12:21, 24-28: _____

3. Exodus 20:8-10: _____

4. II Samuel 6:20: _____

5. Joshua 24:15: _____

6. Acts 16:15: _____

7. Acts 21:8, 9: _____

8. I Corinthians 16:15: _____

9. II Timothy 4:19: _____

10. Romans 16:10-13: _____

B. State how the following verses suggest a family may serve God together.

1. Deuteronomy 16:11, 14: _____

2. Deuteronomy 29:10, 11: _____

3. Joshua 8:34, 35: _____

4. Acts 10:24-33: _____

5. Romans 16:15: _____

6. I Corinthians 16:15: _____

7. Acts 18:24-28: _____

8. III John 1-6: _____

9. Mark 2:14, 15: _____

10. Hebrews 13:2: _____

11. Matthew 25:34-36: _____

12. I Peter 3:7: _____

C. Make a list of the ways that your family will serve Christ.

1. _____

2. _____

3. _____

4. _____

5. _____

6. _____

7. _____

8. _____

9. _____

10. _____

WORKSHEET FOR SONS OR DAUGHTERS, NO. I

1. How would you describe your relationship with each of your parents? Describe your relationship as excellent (5), very good (4), good (3), fair (2), poor (1), terrible (0).

2. On a separate sheet of paper, write down:
   a. Your reasons for rating your relationship as you did;
   b. What has helped or hindered your relationship;
   c. What could be done by you to improve your relationship.

3. Put yourself in the place of your parents and imagine what you would want from a child if you were they. What would you want a child to be? to do for you? How would you want your child to respond to you, or to listen to you, to talk to you, to cooperate with you, to communicate and share with you? Make a list and then ask yourself if their expectations are reasonable or unreasonable. Are there ways in which you should change to become a better child? If so, how?

4. Write down the word "father" and then list everything that is good and worthy of respect about him. Think of character traits, attitudes, actions, relationships, activities. Think of every aspect of his life: physical, spiritual, mental, marital, familial, social, verbal, communal, financial, recreational, personal, etc. Continue to add to this list. Make it a practice to look regularly for the good things in your father's life. Communicate your appreciation to him regularly, specifically, and enthusiastically. Do the same thing for your mother.

5. Make a list of at least 10 fun things that each parent enjoys that you can enjoy with him/her. Ask them to do these things with you, and let them know you really want to be with them. Plan to spend time with your parents regularly.

6. How would you describe the communication level of your family? Use the scale listed under question 1.

7. What are the hindrances to your communication with your parents? List them.

8. Is there a parent with whom you have a greater difficulty? What can you do to break through the communication barrier with this person? How can you improve the communication level with this person?

9. List at least 15 ways that you do or can show love to your parents. Think especially in terms of your parents' desires, likes, and dislikes. Put the list into practice immediately and continuously.

10. Using the following list as headings, list three items under each heading in order of priority as you think your mother and father would respond: chief joys, disappointments, goals or aspirations, likes, dislikes, interests, concerns, problems.

WORKSHEET FOR SONS OR DAUGHTERS, NO. 2

1. Make a detailed list describing your understanding of a son's or daughter's responsibility to his/her parents. Ask not what should my parents do for me, but what should I do for my parents? What are my responsibilities to them? Be specific and comprehensive. Include the whole sphere of your life and theirs; include your responsibilities in the area of actions, attitudes, time, conversation, sharing, etc.

2. Make a list of the following Scripture verses on a separate sheet of paper and then study each one to determine how God wants you to respond and relate to your parents. Some of the passages deal directly with child-parent relations; others with how we should relate to people in general. These latter passages, of course, are particularly relevant in reference to parents. Scripture (I Tim. 5:4) says that we should first learn to rightly relate to and care for our family. We should learn to rightly relate to all men, but first in order of importance should be the members of our own family. Scripture (I Tim. 5:4-8) indicates that failure to do so has serious implications.

   Exodus 20:12; Leviticus 19:3; Proverbs 1:8, 9; 4:1; 6:20-22; 11:29; 13:1; 15:20; 17:6, 25; 22:28; 23:22-25; 28:24; 30:17; Romans 1:28-32; 13:1-10; I Corinthians 6:1-3; Ephesians 6:1-3; Philippians 2:1-4; Colossians 3:20.

3. In the Bible God gives certain promises to children who obey Him in reference to their parents.
   a. List the promises found in the following verses: Exodus 20:12; Proverbs 1:8, 9; 4:1, 2; 6:20-22; Ephesians 6:1-3.
   b. God promises that the child who honors his parents will be blessed—"that it may be well with you" (Eph. 6:3). Make a list of ways that children who honor their parents are often blessed. (Two suggestions to get started: statistics demonstrate that children who have a good relationship with their parents are much more likely to have happy, fulfilling marriages; they are better adjusted and free to use their emotional and mental energy for constructive purposes—they are not controlled and consumed by resentment and bitterness against and reaction to their parents. This sets them free to really be productive and constructive.)

4. In the Bible God also issues warnings to children who disobey Him in reference to their parents.
   a. List the warnings found in the following verses: Proverbs 28:24; 30:17; Romans 1:28-32; I Timothy 5:8; Mark 7:8-13; Galatians 6:7.
   b. Think about some of the ways that a son or daughter who dishonors his/her parents may suffer for it. (For example, Galatians 6:7 indicates

that he/she should not be surprised if his/her own children relate to him/her exactly as he/she related to his/her parents, only worse.)

5. Two words that are frequently used in reference to a child's responsibility to his parents are "obey" and "honor."
   a. Make a list of what your parents expect of you in every aspect of life—at home, school, spiritually, speech, attitudes, dating, etc.
   b. Do you obey your parents in everything? (Col. 3:20).

   Give two examples of times when you obeyed your parents even though you really did not want to obey.

   Give two examples of times or areas in which you have not or are not obeying them.
   c. Do you honor your parents? (This involves attitude and spirit as well as actions and behavior; when you show disrespect, stubbornness, ingratitude, uncooperativeness, resentment, bitterness, disdain, or contempt, you are not honoring your parents.) Do your parents and others know that you really appreciate and respect them? Examine your attitudes and speech; what you don't do as well as what you do when you answer this question.
   d. Plan at least 10 ways to honor your parents. Begin to put the list into practice immediately.

6. Proverbs 10:1 says that "a wise son [daughter] makes a father glad, but a foolish son [daughter] is a grief to his mother."
   a. List some ways you make your parents glad.
   b. List some things about you that bring them grief.
   c. How could you change to bring them more joy and happiness? Examine your attitude, speech, behavior, use of money, time, habits, etc.